THE DIGITIZED CITY:
INFLUENCE & IMPACT

BY CHARLES LANDRY

in collaboration with
City of Helsinki Urban Facts

First published by Comedia in the UK in 2016

ISBN: 978-1-908777-06-5

Comedia The Round, Bournes Green Near Stroud, GL6 7NL, UK

Book design: **www.hillsdesign.co.uk**

All photographs: **Charles Landry** unless otherwise stated

Cover photograph: *Lyons: The spectacular Fête des Lumières is a digital light feast and photo opportunity*

The Comedia Shorts series are all available from: **www.charleslandry.com**

01: The Origins & Futures of the Creative City. ISBN: 978-1-908777-00-3
02: The Sensory Landscape of Cities. ISBN: 978-1-908777-01-0
03: The Creative City Index with Jonathan Hyams ISBN: 978-1-9087770-02-7
04: Culture & Commerce ISBN: 978-1-908777-03-4
05: The Fragile City & the Risk Nexus with Tom Burke ISBN 978-1-908777-04-1
06: Cities of Ambition ISBN 978-1-908777-05-8

Printed on FSC certified paper, using fully sustainable, vegetable oil-based inks, power from 100% renewable resources and waterless printing technology.

Sydney: Sitting on the floor can be a third place at the Museum of Contemporary Art.

CONTENTS

Summary	5
Preface	8
Overture	11
Gutenberg 3.0	11
A third platform	12
Transformations & simulations	13
The city an actor	14
Aims & intent	17
The city of humans	17
Policy priorities	19
The digital universe	25
Digimodernism	25
Dynamics of digitization	26
Volume, velocity, variety	26
The Internet of Things	27
The city is software	29
Cognitive load & overload	30
The visual & the verbal	31

The urban experience 35
  The seductive city 35
  The sensescape of cities 35
    Art & commerce 37
  The smart city 38
    The citizen centre-stage 40
  Foresight & weak signals 42
  The collaborative imperative 45

Delights & discontents 47
    The promise, paradoxes & predicaments 47
  Openness & the innovation accelerator 48
    Open source 48
    Sci-art & the digital 49
    Experiment zones & living labs 49
  The social & the shared 51
    Anytime, anyplace, anywhere 53
    The power of place & third places 53
  Encroachment & engagement 56
    A bias to be social 57
    Chemistry & curiosity 58
    Storytelling 60

Governance & democracy 63
  The end of open-ended openness 63
    MyData – the Nordic model 64
  Reinventing democracy 64
    Harnessing community intelligence 65
  The mobile citizen 67

Measuring the digital eco-system 69

Digital literacy 73

Highlighted issues
  Acronym overload 15
  The power of BlindSquare 18
  The API economy & seamless connectivity 22
  The City of Things 28
  The pioneer 41
  Civility & etiquette 61
  Transparency & governance 65

THE DIGITIZED CITY: INFLUENCE & IMPACT

Summary

The digitized city is already with us, but it needs a jointly created vision of where next. Digitization represents a tectonic shift providing computing with an immense force. Its devices are changing society and social life, culture, levels of connectivity, the economy as well as cities. These devices are both liberating and potentially invasive.

The impacts and influence of the digital age are vastly stronger than some tinkering on top of business as usual. They will be as powerful as the climactic changes that swept through our world with the industrial revolution 200 years ago. That revolution had powerful symbols of giant turbines and whirring machines whereas this one is more invisible with its small screens and changing images.

Digitization will be as powerful in its effects as the industrial revolution 200 years ago.

This movement concerns us all and the open data agenda, smart city ideas or evolving collaborative governance models are just some responses to this bigger dynamic unfolding.

Undeniably untold promises and opportunities to improve our quality of life are possible by making life more citizen centric, more local, more convenient or efficient and by creating smart solutions to curtail energy over-use or crafting ingenious ways to enable seamless connectivity. Filling the city with self-regulating sensors brings real time feedback loops into their own.

Yet these positives mesh as with all new technologies with dangers. Here being controlled by algorithms or the ever watchful eye of surveillance or suffering overload of constant data cascading over us and unemployment created by the power of intelligent robots are the most pressing.

The sophisticated merging of computing power and vast archives of data will enable robots to perform any job that is predictable and increasingly hollow out middle income employment – a group that so far was largely unscathed[1].

We are in the midst of redesigning the world and all its systems – legal, moral and political as well as the economy and our infrastructures for a digital age with ICT as one backbone. The crucial question is: 'will the public interest be put centre-stage'.

Our built environment has been designed for how we lived and worked 50 years ago and more. A reverse engineering process is necessary to adapt to the digital age as well as to create new infrastructures that live within its hard-engineered fabric.

Place matters as never before in spite of our increased virtual interactions as people need physical place to anchor themselves in. The public realm rises dramatically in importance and as working patterns change gathering places and especially third spaces have renewed relevance.

The volume, velocity and variety of instantly available data streams combined the 'anytime, anyplace, anywhere' phenomenon changes how we interact with space, place and time.

The redesign of the emergent city needs bigger values that place us humans at the centre and a linked urban culture to anchor its actions. A human perspective should drive technologies rather than technologies shaping our potential. Crucially the innovative impulses unleashed should also seek to solve old problems with new economy possibilities such as addressing inequality or creating quality jobs.

Cities, citizens and the variety of urban leaders have a once in a lifetime opportunity to rebuild our cities in a different way, including harnessing the capabilities of social media, interactive platforms or open data to deepen democracy and to make it more engaging and responsive to peoples' desires and needs. This cannot happen in the tried and already tested ways and a new level of openness is essential.

Cities need to remain alert to ensure their priorities and values are acknowledged as the digital industrial complex has discovered the city as a major new market. In addition the communications revolution has broken the public sector data monopoly as everyone has access to knowledge on their devices and as well can be an editor of their own media.

Cities need a 'thinking brain' combining public, private and citizen interests to scan the horizon to monitor and to understand the

> The emergent digitized city needs ethical values to guide its progress with human beings placed centre-stage.

Google: Is our once hip friend now too powerful and sucking everything into its orbit.

emerging signals and innovations. This mixed partnership needs an agile organizational form. Perhaps the lead public sector entity could be the research and statistical departments with a reinvented remit and foresight role as well as additional skills.

Collaborative models based on openness are key to survive well in this emerging world. It requires a new governance model whose co-creation effect could be just as disruptive as Uber was to taxi companies. Redefining the city as a community of brains is a different paradigm whose aim is to harness the collective community intelligence for the common good.

To keep the best of this innovation dynamic and to avoid the pitfalls requires some policy priorities, which include: a MyData agenda to safeguard privacy and allowing people to manage their own data; to be continually alert to balance public and private benefits; to foster a new civic culture that is determined to be co-creative; to create rules and codes for the sensorized city, the city of interactive surfaces and immersive digital environments based on open standards and architectures[2] ; to invest in digital literacy so we are capable of understanding what is going on and finally to be alert to the dangers of our lives being controlled by algorithms.

Preface

The digitized city: Influence & Impact is not written for those well versed as experienced aficionados of the Internet, mobile technology or smart-city thinking. It is targeted not at the tech savvy but instead at the rest of us interested in the emergent world of digitally driven and enabled cities and how these cities will evolve and affect us as citizens, businesses and the public sector.

Its origin lies in a symposium called '**Harnessing Knowledge for the City**' held in Helsinki. It focused on how we will experience, navigate and understand the digitized, sensorized city whose deeper impacts are yet to unfold as the power of big data and intelligent objects emerges with greater force.

Citizens and city leaders cannot avoid being involved to ensure we collectively harness the benefits of technology as disruptive user-driven business models supplying a constant cascade of information have changed the way cities work. Airbnb is in effect a hotel chain without hotels, where Uber allows everyone to be a taxi driver and where daily commentary on facilities and places allows TripAdvisor to be a constant companion.

Many of these innovations are immensely helpful and popular, yet they challenge existing interests.

These are of special interest to public entities whose public data providers and statistical offices have for a century held a near monopoly on information. That monopoly no longer exists and ironically their desire to open up their data is helping to break down their own strong positions as activists, as the business world and others embrace the resulting digital opportunities.

Meanwhile, much of the public sector does not benefit from or even bother to understand these new opportunities. Neither do they understand the value their own activities and data might be enabling. Two different worlds are emerging that presently do not match, yet there are mutual opportunities if both parties were clever enough to explore options together.

The digitized city: Influence & Impact could not have been written without the knowledge and insights of the participants at the Symposium as well as others who were consulted elsewhere. They are in alphabetical order:

Pieter Ballon, director, iMinds, Flanders; Timo Cantell, director, City of Helsinki Urban Facts; Karl-Filip Coenegrachts, chief strategy officer, City of Ghent; Jarmo Eskelinen, managing director, Forum Virium Helsinki; Dan Hill, director of Future Cities, Catapult and now Arups, London; Ari Jaakola, statistics manager Helsinki Urban Facts; Nikolaos Kontinakis, project co-ordinator knowledge society, Eurocities, Brussels; Tanja Lahti, project manager, Helsinki Region Infoshare; Christopher Lindinger, director R&I, Ars Electronica Linz; Ville Meloni, Digital Helsinki, project manager; Veera Mustonen, Kalasatama project manager, Helsinki; Maarit Palo, business development executive IBM Finland; Ikka Pirttimaa CTO, Founder, MIPSoft / BlindSquare; Antti Poikola, My Data activist; Manel Sanroma; CEO, Barcelona Circles; Pekka Sauri, vice-mayor Helsinki; Marco Steinberg, founder, Snowcone & Haystack; Teemu Vass, coordinator Helsinki Urban Facts; Ritva Viljanen, vice-mayor Helsinki; Katja Vilkama, research director Helsinki Urban Facts. In addition Davor Meersman, director City of Things, Antwerp; Peter Finnegan, director international relations, Dublin City Council and Jonathan Hyams, founder Artlook Software.

> Citizens and city leaders must be collaborative to ensure collective benefits ensue.

Waiting Time

About 15 Minutes

from this point

인천국제공항출입국관리사무소
INCHEON AIRPORT
IMMIGRATION OFFICE

INCHEON AIRPORT IMMUNOPA

OVERTURE

Remember the world not long ago without digital connectivity. Consider these days doing research without the vast electronic library that is the Internet, without instant messaging, without social media, without feedback loops.

Remember how fixing a date had to be firm and specific rather than flexible and fluid, or the query that took you to the local library where searching the card catalogue was a chore and often an inter-library loan sorted it out - after quite a wait. Life did not run as we currently know it.

Stark reminders of this quite recent and very different world come to us from crises and from our awareness of restrictive regimes. Hurricane Sandy caused Internet outages lasting days and brought to mind the iconic images of bereft people trying to connect or even just to recharge phones and laptops. Visiting China if your account is Gmail or Hotmail effectively disconnects you from your world. The instant transactions are gone. Things are no longer ubiquitous and immediate.

Consider too the contrast in life experience and perception between those born native into the digital world, the Generation Z kids, and those older people - who still make most of our decisions – who have had to adapt to it.

Gutenberg 3.0

At the core of the vast changes affecting every facet of our lives lies digitization and its power to connect, to communicate and to manipulate data. There is a data mining revolution. It is an innovation accelerator. It is the Gutenberg of our era and has engendered similarly powerful effects. It has transformed how we work, how we manage and organize, what we do, how we create, and even how we think. Digitally driven tools and technologies shape how and what we produce and consume and how we experience the world.

Our culture is digital and it is the digital that shapes our culture. The digital allowed a revolution in the use of information and is now like the air we breathe and the electricity that flows – it is

oul: The digital
e can create a
enzied, speedy
orld.

omni-present. It shifts people's understanding of time, space, and place. Who would have thought that one set of discoveries would create a new world shaped through electrical signals of zeros and ones, ons and offs, or trues and falses. Or that the power of the binary code would be so dramatically different from the analogue world with its electrical signals transmitted using wave forms continuously modulating their strength, their sound vibrations or varying their frequency. Communication was largely one-way as in the classic radio or TV.

The move from an analogue to a digital world at first took time to unfold, and while both continue to co-exist, the digital gathered speed and has been quite sudden, all-pervasive and climactic in its effects.

Two linked breakthroughs from the early 1990s enhanced the power of the digital: connecting mobile systems and computers wirelessly; and miniaturizing transistors (as encapsulated by Moore's Law) so vastly increasing computing power. With wireless technology, the need to build the billions of kilometres of physical cables is mitigated.

A third platform

The digital now rides on its third platform. The first was the era of mainframes and terminals. The second was the period of laptops driven largely by a client/server relationship where messages are exchanged in a request-response pattern. The combination of the cloud, mobile devices, social media and big data technologies working together are creating a new platform. Here mobile devices and apps extend capabilities, here the cloud acts as an outsourced mechanism, here big data enables ultra-fast analysis to interpret data and to gain insights and social technologies bring interactive human dimensions into digital, automated processes. It is the mashing of these disparate technologies and breaking the silos that is turbocharging digital commerce, information analytics and the development of intelligent infrastructures. Google, Amazon or Facebook, Uber, Airbnb and Twitter have used these to powerful effect. These digital winners and the myriad of start-ups institutionalize their disruption-seeking radars and antennae[3]. It is the scope, scale, pervasiveness, the ubiquity and speed that the evolving technologies enable that is astonishing. And remember there were only a few million mainframe users in its time while now 2.5 billion people are connected to the Internet.

The Internet – with its connective effects powered by the World Wide Web's ability to help share information – created the terms in which we talk about the world and its projects like 'smart cities', 'open data movement' or 'The Internet of Things'. Work and its processes and collaborations could not have been so easy or smooth without the existence of these networks.

The watchwords are open, fluid, flexible, interactive, co-creative, agile, connective, instant, immersive, ubiquitous, enabling, sharing, integrative, multitasking, simulated, virtual, fragmenting, fracturing and constantly online.

Connectivity and networking is the backbone of the digital age. (by rawpixel.com)

Transformations & simulations

Paradigm shift is a concept to be used sparingly. Yet there are moments and movements when the idea is apt, and full-blown digitization and its capacity to simulate and virtualize experience is one. Indeed it is the most crucial topic in contemporary culture – the mental and social transformation created by our new electronic environment that allows us too to blend and mix the 'virtual' and the 'real'. Simulated products, services and augmented reality experiences are extending everywhere even creating virtual social networks, relationships and feelings. Why fall in love with a real person and its attendant difficulties when I can invent emotions? Or why play football outside when I can use my XBOX? The link between reality, symbols, and society were questions Jean Baudrillard already presciently examined in the early 1980's in 'Simulacra and Simulations'[4].

Our data drenched world enables transformation on a scale that changes the foundations of business and public service and even our lives sweeping the ground from under their feet shaking up everything from operating models to their infrastructure. Its effects are all-embracing touching every function and process from how to communicate, to engage, to market, to sell. It is more than business as usual with a bit of tinkering.

Bari: Four old guys contempl[
whether this changing worl[
anything to offer [

Dramatic transformation does not happen by choice, mostly. That is too difficult since attitudes, behaviours and systems entrench and the tried and tested dominates over what could be. It is forced upon us by crisis, by opportunities being missed, by technological potential, by others doing better.

Discovered by science, further explored and exploited by industry, the digital opened untold opportunities as business searched for new ways of staying competitive and getting ahead of rivals. In this process a new market was discovered for digital solutions and products and services – the city.

The city an actor

Consider the effect on and possibilities for cities and how they feel and are experienced from how we navigate space, the impact of responsive, interactive digitized screens, to how we shop and how we transition from the virtual to the real and back again and how these blend and what this does to our behaviour. It creates too the possibilities for a 'smarter city' from the simple to the complex. You know when the next bus or metro is coming to where a free car parking space is, yet more powerfully self-regulating mechanisms help us find where we are, enable us to control our energy use or monitor levels of pollution and much more. It creates easier feedback loops between citizens and the city decision makers and so in principle can help us reinvigorate local democracy. It allows the idea of the 'sharing economy' to be possible, which is built around sharing human and physical resources, it fosters swapping, exchanging or joint purchasing. Car sharing technology, like ZipCars is a prime example.

At some level as Dan Hill notes 'The past is the future' as the technology allows us to recapture the lost threads of locality. We can become more local with the power of distributed systems from energy to mobility, to decision making in urban planning and development.

Such dramatic changes affect us viscerally. At times they engender fear that the world is racing ahead of us, uncontrolled. At others it spawns excitement about the manifold opportunities unfolding. Those who are older remember the analogue world and have experienced the increasing influence and impact of the digital. They have had to migrate into this world whereas for the young it is all they know. Yet for all of us there is a shadow side when being ever present and online can overwhelm, can fragment and can disturb our focus. Remember that great places have some important key features: they are places of anchorage with a sense of stability; places of possibility; places of connection; of learning; and of inspiration. Some of this the digitized city provides and some it does not.

Acronym overload

New worlds require new language and the techie words that dominate our mental landscape can confuse. While the uninitiated just about understand open data they wonder what a data ocean or data lake, a data graveyard, or meta data or meta data of meta data could be. There is a danger of acronym overload as new words and concepts enter the vocabulary which most of us do not understand but are vitally important to how life unfolds. Think of SaaS, PaaS, DaaS, IaaS or ITMaaS or API, gamification or cognitive computing. That is "software as a service", "platform as a service", "desktop as a service", "mobile backend as a service" and "information technology management as a service" or "Application Programming Interface". Even the phrase 'smart city' confuses and is contentious. The duty to explain is a democratic priority indeed imperative.

The ordinary person may not understand, but they live with its effects. Digital literacy is then a must as we need new skills and new jobs - think of recent job titles from growth hacker, UX or UI designer, content strategists, to information and data architects. They speak for themselves.

AIMS & INTENT

The city of humans

The digitized city is already with us, but it needs a vision of where next. This emergent city needs bigger values and an urban culture to anchor its actions, to drive its technologies and to solve old problems with new economy possibilities such as addressing inequality or creating quality jobs. It should never start with technology on its own. Technology fever and innovative apps make one forget that it is the enabler and the servant of our objectives and bigger goals. We need to ask who technology serves and for what purposes. It is never neutral. Its directions, its research agendas, the problems its sets out to solve are determined by private and public choices, which are ultimately about values and politics, as is what data we archive and what data we expose to new uses or scrutiny.

... we have a once in a lifetime opportunity to build our cities in a different way.

We now have a once in a lifetime opportunity to build our city in a different way, but this cannot happen with a business as usual approach. It will take time to emerge fully and it needs to be grounded in principles, intent and aims, married to a paced and purposeful approach. We are redesigning the world and all its systems — legal, moral and political, and infrastructures for a digital age with ICT as one backbone. Yet the focus must be on the human as this change should be for more than only efficiency or to save money and to deal with the effects of austerity. At its heart lies openness, an empowering stance that helps unleash untapped talents and capabilities as well as potential locked in silos in both public administrations, private businesses and across sectors.

This central intent can help harness the collective imagination of people to assist them to be the best they can be; so improving their chances of mobilizing their intellectual resources. It should be an empowering process. An engine for this is openness. This is why the open data programme of cities from Helsinki, to Washington to Amsterdam to Berlin was driven largely by the democratic impulse to be transparent since data, our data, was closed and made people feel subservient, passive and even ignorant. 'Give back data to the people themselves for them to be wise or smart'

ntwerp: Digital
izardry shows
olidarity for the
aris outrages of 13th
ovember 2015 at
he Museum aan de
room.

The Power of BlindSquare

Ilkka Pirttimaa invented BlindSquare a potent tool for the visually impaired in reverse order. He started by pondering how you could put together existing open data reserves with the new features of smartphones. His idea was to combine the huge geodata resources of Foursquare and the Open Street Map with possibilities offered by the speech synthesis functions of smartphones. He had no end user in mind and had not yet met a single visually impaired person.

Then it clicked and Pirttimaa realized the potential for the visually impaired of bringing GPS and sound together and created an accessible GPS-app that describes the environment as you travel, announcing points of interest and street intersections. To constantly improve and update the software he familiarized himself with the daily lives of the visually impaired by reading their blogs and now over twenty around the world are testing the beta version of BlindSquare. Pirttimaa has received so many ideas from beta testers and other BlindSquare users for the development of the service that over 50 new features have been added to the service in six months, based on the feedback. The users also chose the name for the application.

It can help you avoid falling down some stairs in a shopping centre or help you find the right classroom on a campus or spot the water slide in a water park. It can even help the blind/deaf by linking them to a Braille display or tell you where you are on a moving vehicle.

Thanks to its global data sources BlindSquare can be used anywhere and has users in over 50 countries. In Helsinki the application has added the city's service map, such as the accessibility of libraries and the region's real time transport information in addition to Foursquare and the Open Street Map. Other cities are starting to follow this example in using local public data. Anecdotes best express BlindSquare's usefulness, such as the feedback Pirttimaa received from a Canadian user who said they can now go somewhere alone for the first time in 64 years.

... new technologies always pose dilemmas. Does the digital engage or encroach.

was a clarion call, and its vast and powerful side-effects enhanced both the problem-solving capacities of communities and also of businesses adding value to products and services. This is what people mean by wanting 'smart citizens' in a 'smart city'.

Technology is that double-edged sword with advances often creating and posing binary dilemmas, such as does it facilitate or control, does it open things out or close them off, do its commercial conveniences and its voracious data gathering and continuous tracking invade my privacy or provide public opportunities, does it encroach or engage, does its all-embracing connectivity enhance my relationships and depth of understanding or flatten them and

Constantly available and ever online.
(by rawpixel.com).

make them shallow. The trajectory of travel and its journey is clear towards the more open, the more public, more enabling, but it needs a social stance buttressed by a legal and regulatory framework to match in order to protect its benefits.

The Internet's origins and ethos as a shared networking platform for scientific research remains an ideal. This is mirrored by the open data movement instigated by cities – indeed it is our data since gathering it was paid by taxes. Yet a tension is emerging between citizens or companies as users of public data and the devouring and insatiable Internet search engines who in essence invade our private lives by capturing every move we make, especially online. This spells the end of open-ended openness.

Policy priorities

Cities, and their public entities, must be active players in this emergent city, both shaping it and being shaped by it. They need to balance regulating with enabling, and the setting of promotional standards with incentivizing. They need to be pioneers and experimenters as well as to encourage development by procurement. They need to assess the public

interest issues at stake and lobby for the balance between privacy and openness. Yet their default position must be openness, as from this transparency the innovative dynamics grow. This highlights the priority for public policy jointly conceived and co-created including:

MyData: The privacy agenda is rising in importance and here a 'Mydata' infrastructure is required to enable the individual to manage their own data. This moves the default position on making data gathering choices away from corporates.

Balancing interests: Cities have to be continually alert to ensure the balance of public and private benefits. As the search for new markets saw the city as a target for digital solutions a new risk has emerged as companies realise the value and close data again. Citymapper, for instance, is based on open data from Transport for London (TfL) and it has enabled a refined picture of how citizens move around the city – but only Citymapper knows this is and TfL has to buy back this strategic data to make decisions about developing their service.

Co-creating the city: A new city is emerging that superficially looks the same – there are streets, pavements, buildings and parks, but its operating dynamic is different. This changing context makes us ask what purpose do public administration and city institutions

serve, and question what they should it be providing for citizens especially when some services are created and driven by the very citizens themselves. This requires a different bureaucracy that is deeply enabling, seeing its citizens and businesses as partners in a joint city making endeavour.

This new 'civic city' will have a new form including a slimmer administration as well as new departments currently unknown to us. Indeed the departments handling data interpretation or interactions may rise dramatically in importance. Classic silo working becomes redundant in this context as information and interactions are horizontal issues affecting every sphere.

Some say the city is a 'concentration of dense human interactions in place and time'. A central role for public entities is to monitor, interpret and balance these interactions and transactions, which mostly embody power relations, between the public entities, its community, companies and individuals as interactions with citizens can be lost (see the Citymapper example).

There are vast opportunities to both improve and re-create the city, but like with all innovations the answer is unknown in advance. This implies an organisational ethos that enables an experimentation culture and the city and its citizens are the big arenas to test this out. Just like the R&D departments of companies the city needs one with strategic principles about the kind of place it wants to be and tactically flexible in trying to get there. Living Labs allow you to practice a more innovative society in reality without stopping you in its tracks when some things inevitably go wrong. These labs can be buildings, streets, neighbourhoods or even the complete city, as with the City of Things project in Antwerp. (see box)

There are vast opportunities to get the digitally enabled city right if the policies are in place.

This professional and managed testing culture requires tools and processes of experimentation to harness community power and business creativity. A culture of experimentation is a good bridge between these actors. What then are the roles for organisations like Urban Facts in Helsinki or OIS in Amsterdam formerly fact producing machines? With digitalisation there is something more they could do such as being a neutral interpreter or thinking brain for the city.

Standards & codes: Rules and standards for the sensorized city, are needed. The city of interactive surfaces and immersive digital environments where everything is malleable, can over – communicate and overload the senses. Much is useful information, but at a critical point it can turn into visual pollution. Think here of what is already happening in theme parks, in the casinos of Macau or Las Vegas, 42nd Street New York, in retail environments and the billboards in our cities, which unchecked can consume the visual landscape with cities 'suffocating under a smog of signage'. First São Paulo and then Chennai banned billboards and now Grenoble is developing areas for public expression and has replaced 326 advertising signs with community noticeboards and trees, and others like Paris are following in their footsteps with Tehran replacing its ads with art for 10 days. The movements to control our visual environments are escalating raising questions about our collective urban experience. Yet the city provides endless

... codes are also needed for digitally enabled visual pollution.

The API economy & seamless connectivity

Connectivity needs connectors and interfaces between differing softwares were historically the blockage. Application Programming Interfaces (APIs) unlock the obstacles and they are like a door or a window. They have become more than a piece of technology to being elevated as a driver of the business models and roadmaps of the digital economy. They are the catalyst and backbone that is force feeding the next wave of opportunities as products in themselves not just enablers and are a fundamental building block for the Internet of Things. APIs integrate programmes and define how they interact with the rest of the software world so creating competitive advantages and leveraging possibilities. New specialists will emerge, such as the 'cross-functional project manager' who can weave together various systems into a compelling business offer.

APIs allow the mix and match to enable sprawling web-services from Google to Facebook to talk to each other so defining the web experience with their convenience and ability to save time. When you search for a restaurant in the Yelp app it plots their locations on Google Maps instead of creating its own maps. Equally the icons you see to share on article on Facebook, Google+, Twitter, LinkedIn or Reddit are based on APIs. Foursquare, as an example recently announced that its API now has 10,000 registered developers. Yet the openness APIs provide is under threat as Twitter or Google, for instance, are limiting third party applications' use of their APIs, forcing users to use their sites. Twitter aims to monetize clicks by displaying ads and promoted tweets insisting this is necessary to provide a "unified" Twitter experience.

https://www2.deloitte.com/content/dam/Deloitte/us/Documents/financial-services/us-fsi-api-economy.pdf opportunities to satisfy the thirst for commercial communication such as tracking devices hidden in recycling bins[5].

And think of shops as they turn into experience centres as they need to offer something extra over online purchasing, which is of course cheaper as it cuts out the middleman. The concept stores like Ferrari or Audi or Abercrombie & Fitch are a mere harbinger of things to come. Remember too that the Internet shifts and exports the hard labour onto you. You buy the ticket not the travel agent, you explore and purchase the fridge rather than someone helping you all in the name of choice. And 'contact us' means electronically as it becomes increasingly difficult to speak to a human voice. The same occurred with the rise of supermarkets. This is why personal service and advice is at such a premium.

Digital literacy: This is a sine-qua-non for a competent citizen in the digital age and these e-skills include the ability to find, evaluate, utilize, share, and create content using information technologies and the Internet. Equally there is a need to understand the digital universe and its history, its drivers, its key terms from APIs to the slippery smart city idea as well as digital economics and its social impacts.

Algorithmic control: Finally, the digital is opaque. It needs to explain itself and a role of public entities is to make its processes transparent as well as find ways to make the invisible visible as only then can people participate and engage as capable, empowered citizens.

... Our lives being controlled by algorithms is one of the great dangers to freedom in our era.

Algorithms behind the scenes control everything we do on the web and they are closely guarded commercial secrets. Getting a loan – an algorithm looks at your bank records and decides without human intervention. Dating – an algorithm sifts through characteristics to give you a perfect match. What books you might read or films to watch, what you might buy, all can be calculated and it is cookies that help this process. These algorithms help sift through data ultra-fast to determine whether you are a security threat, while they also can be used to spy on you. They are 'the maths that help computers decide stuff'[6]. They are invisible computations that increasingly determine how we interact with the electronic world. No wonder we need to know as a matter of public policy.

Tickets.
Platforms.
Times.
All at my
fingertips.
I am train.

trainline

THE DIGITAL UNIVERSE

Connectivity and data are the new forms of capital, supplanting material resources, finance or location, and they have enabled and fast tracked the digital revolution and the disruption of established business models.

Its twin engines are the Internet's massive networks of networked computers rapidly accelerated by the widespread adoption of browsers and World Wide Web technology. This allows users easy access to information linked throughout the globe where protocols such as TCP/IP are vital in defining how computers, servers and networks route data. The dominant protocol, TCP/IP gave the Internet its 'interconnecticity' and our feeling that the web is a fluid space.

Digimodernism

"The cultural landscape is skewed at all times by the gravitational pull of certain ideas, themes, tendencies or individuals... and the one which is gradually bending everything into its orbit as well as throwing up phenomena made in its own image, is digitization". This landscape Alan Kirby calls *digimodernism*[7]. It is becoming the dominant cultural force of the 21st century and is displacing the empty shell and exhausted ideas of post-modernism, which now offers little in terms of explanatory power or innovation potential. Digimodernism's meaning centres on the impact of computers on all forms of culture and art and on how words and texts are written, used and placed, such as in the web 2.0 of blogs, chat rooms, message boards, Wikipedia, Facebook or Twitter. Here technology is like oxygen and increasingly easy to use. This in turn affects our mindscape, our perceptions, our ways of analyzing and thinking and ultimately what we do and how we behave. We cannot avoid it and we are pulled into its thrall with its fluid, evanescent, malleable, remixed content, in which we graze (the digital form of what we once called browsing) and dive deep and where its 'spatial boundaries are perceptible, but very hard to fix'. This reminds us that writing a letter or using an atlas to find your way or booking a ticket at an office are rarities and that researching, learning and education have transformed as have making payments, entertaining oneself, dating and searching for a job.

ondon metro:
he convenience
martphones
rovide is
tonishing.

This digital landscape is apparently a free for all and open though furtively patrolled by what Dan Hill calls the 'Urban Intelligence Industrial Complex' led by IBM, Cisco, General Electric, Siemens, Philips and search engines like Google or Yahoo[8].

Dynamics of digitization

Volume, velocity, variety

Within this digital universe the three big game-changers are: big data, the Internet of Things, and intelligent objects. Crucially for city decision makers the power of big data and its associated algorithms lies in its capacity to move from a 'descriptive to predictive and prescriptive analytics' and doing data analysis in real-time[9]. Seen as the 'final frontier of analytical capabilities' it automatically synthesizes data with mathematical and computer sciences to make both predictions and then to make recommendations for decision making. Descriptive analytics looks at past performance and trends and predictive analytics tries to assess the likelihood of what will happen. How much room is there then for autonomous judgement based on more subjective factors?

Add to this the defining dimension of big data and its 'volume, velocity, and variety' enabled by the Internet and a powerful resource is being unleashed. Having eliminated the classic trade-off between the amount of information shared and the number of people you can share it with, the Internet makes all those public entities and companies who are stuck in closed environments vulnerable.

The vast information mass that makes up the evolving digital universe is made up of texts, images and videos on mobile phones, You Tube uploads, digital movies, banking data swiped in an ATM, security footage, recordings on highway tolls, calls zipping down digital phone lines. It is predicted to grow by 40% each year over the next five years and is barely charted and evaluated with only 3% tagged and ½% analysed according to IDC[10]. A immense task lies ahead for cities, companies, communities and citizens to find the data, to analyze it and to extract value from the seeming chaos, of as many bits as there are stars in the universe, and then to apply it to solving problems or to create opportunities.

... vast data mountains are being tapped, yet even vaster ones remain to be explored.

FEED
YOUR
RESTLESS
CURIOSITY

Krakow: A new third place carved out of the redundant Forum Hotel.

The Internet of Things

The era of the Internet of Things (IoT) concept brings software and 'intelligence' or artificial intelligence to objects and will reach critical mass within the next five years. Devices are beginning to detect gesture, voice and emotion and becoming more contextually aware. The body itself can become an 'Internet of Oneself' monitored 24/7. The concept of the 'quantified self' incorporates technology and aims to provide data streams on most aspects of a person's daily life, such as food consumed, the quality of air, the state of mind such as moods or oxygen levels and the body's performance, such as tracking insulin. This self-monitoring and self-sensing enabled by wearable computers goes by different names, such as lifelogging, self-tracking, auto-analytics or body hacking. The Economist amusingly entitled one of its articles 'the quantified serf'.

... from the quantified self to the quantified city.

The City of Things

A unique quadruple helix based partnership has been set up by iMinds, the Flemish government's ICT research institute; the City of Antwerp; Mobile Vikings, an innovative mobile provider and citizens. This local innovation platform aims to bring the Internet of Things to life. It seeks to create an enabling environment to link open data provided by the city and others as well as open innovation processes that rely on sharing insights and knowledge and that stimulate co-creation. Together the city of Antwerp and its citizens then act as the living lab and real-life test bed. Here users, service providers and producers can jointly develop innovations in a trusted, open ecosystem that spurs business innovations. This closely networked system provides instant feedback loops to research behaviour and to monitor results as well as the technological capacities to respond to issues and to innovate along the way. To drive the process the partnership together provides awards and sets up challenges.

The city is treated as a shared resource by the partners, with each providing rich data sets, for instance the city through its open data policies and Mobile Viking customers via their daily smartphone usage.   In addition there is the technological capacity to gather and analyse user and sensor data with an infrastructure to involve, track, and interact with users at a very large scale (1000s upon 1000s). This platform has multiple connection gateways from Wi-FI to Bluetooth to LoRa, and Zigbee and well beyond so providing an integrated communication system. Thus there is a network layer, a data layer and business layer to the project.

The target groups are broad including the City itself, start-ups and SMEs who can use Antwerp as an experimentation lab and researchers in academia, technology, business and the social domain.

Practically this means citizens and the city can check the health of the environment, mobility patterns, lighting systems or physical problems in a street in real time and through rewards systems direct behaviour to stated goals. These could be to use more bikes and less cars to reduce congestion or pollution. The city could even track stolen traffic cones apparently a large problem. It enables too buildings to become intelligent and instead of being consumers of energy become producers or instead of creating waste make energy out of it.

http://cifal-flanders.org/wp-content/uploads/2015/12/iMinds-City-of-Things-Davor-Meersman-30-11-2015.pdf

... A sensorized city offers novel levels of communication.

These possibilities will allow new forms of interaction and new levels of personalisation, both which a city could track. The city is a vast canvas where billions of these sensorized devices will communicate eco-information, traffic, where parking spaces are free, crime hotspots, service options or urban maintenance issues to data or research centres. Even though this sensorized city largely looks the same it operates and performs differently, and changes how it is experienced and constructed and how we act within it. Think of Airbnb, Zipcar, Uber, Lyft or Bridj and how they have re-conceived hospitality or urban mobility. This connectivity adds up to convenience.

The IoT takes this one step further and is made up of billions of sensorized objects from tractors to fridges or dog collars and is forming part of an ever-expanding digital universe feeding the creation of untold new apps with an intelligence that monitors, evaluates and acts upon data received. Of the estimated 200 billion larger 'things', currently 14 billion are connected and communicating via the Internet and this is estimated to nearly triple by 2020. These 'live' objects can be manipulated, maintained and be managed from a distance opening up potential for public and private entities, particularly given the agility they offer and their ability to track progress say in logistics or to check the health of the system itself. The challenges include that the IoT is intrinsically global and this ease of access requires international operational standards to deal with security issues.

The city is software

The point is being reached where it is possible to say that 'the city is software'. The slogan "software is eating the world"[11] resonates since every firm or public department is in the software business and is a socially-empowered web-centric entity as the global economy will shortly be fully digitally wired. Photography is software enabled through mobiles that upload to the digital universe; Amazon is a software company as its core capability is its software engine able to sell practically everything online. With its reach it hoovers up competitive possibilities and the middleman or retail stores like Borders have gone and with Kindle even books are software. Significantly Amazon's reach continues so that now the system they built for themselves they are selling on as Amazon Web Services, with now over 100 packages. Amazon then is part of the core architecture of organizations, for example like for Stockmann (the biggest department store in Finland), because it is becoming too complex to build your own software or archival systems. In what some call this post-PC world it is like building with LEGO and its modular parts.

... software is the energy flow and nervous system of the city.

Netflix crippled Blockbuster and its software can keep track of every one of its 40 million subscribers. Both Apple's iTunes and Spotify, the biggest music stores, are software driven; the video game makers are software focused; Pixar too. Logistics companies like Fedex or DL are software companies with trucks attached who can monitor everything in real time and adjust to needs along the way; cars are largely software that run engines, safety features and connect the car to mobile, satellite and GPS networks and hybrid and electric cars will be largely computer controlled; practically all financial transactions are executed in software; the success of the oil, gas and mining industries are determined by software. Consider their data visualization and analysis tools needed in exploration and exploitation, which explains why they were the inventors of big data. In short the value chain is shifting from the physical to the software world.

... culture is digital and the digital is. culture.

The question then is not 'what are computers for, but what are they not for', and equally not 'what is digital, but what is not digital'.

The decline of the physical is causing a counter-reaction and the revolt is seen in the *makers' movement*, in which the physical makes a comeback partly because we cannot make or maintain most objects with their high software content.

Significantly this requires new expertise and a new generation of information analyzers, decoders and curators are needed. Are the vocational schools and universities providing the skills?

Cognitive load & sensory overload

There is a shadow side to this potentially glowing picture - the experience of over-stimulation from crowding, noise, media, technology, information bites. Estimates vary[12] but we receive between three to five times as much information than we did 25 years ago and this pales into insignifance with the 100+ fold increase in what we churn out. 295 exabytes of data are floating around the world − that is 29,500,000,000,000,000,000,000 pieces of information[13] representing apparently 315 times the number of grains of sand on Earth. This includes everything from the attention grabbing 'brandscapes' increasingly inhabiting our cityscapes to e-mails, mobiles, twitter and other social media or the video ads on the back of taxi seats, on the bannisters of escalators or uprights of steps in airports or metros to animated ad floor coverings.

There is the burden of choice. On my mobile I can use What's App, texting, calling, Facebook messenger, e-mail, Vine, Snapchat, Instagram, or Twitter, Flickr and LinkedIn. In this world of snippets and facts there are many factoids - items of unreliable information, reported and repeated, they become accepted as fact, to add to the confusion.

A consequence is that we can get over-excited, restless, lack focus and concentration, fiddle, be irritable and ultimately shut out the sounds, impressions and stimuli of flickering lights or mindless white noise much of which is meaningless. The FOMO phenomenon – the fear of missing out – exacerbates this potential frenzy to be ever-present. Add to this cocktail sophisticated neuro-marketing techniques which are constantly assessing how to get deeply into our heads. In sum this can stretch our processing capacity and makes us appear bewildered, unfocused and fragmented and unable to have fine grained interaction.

Overload comes from too much information supplied and too much information demanded plus the need to multi-task to overcome constant interruptions and inadequate personal or external infrastructures to structure our day to day life. The brain is very plastic and good at understanding and processing information, yet being rarely quiet or reflective and always 'on' it is no surprise that the 'mindfulness' trend has grown exponentially.

The visual & the verbal

The world is in the midst of a dramatic transformation from the relatively recent dominance of word and text based communication to the visual. This is profoundly significant for our experience of the city. Digital advances have played a vital part in accelerating this shift with its astonishing capacity to manipulate and bring visual imagery to life, while new image, word and text detecting software enhances possibilities. John Berger noted: "Seeing comes before words"[14].

Indeed since the beginning of our known history the vast majority of our communication was through drawings – think here of cave paintings. Visual symbols were invented 30,000 years ago and writing approximately 5,000 years ago. Imagery is embedded in our primeval brain. Yet the invention of Gutenberg's movable type printing press in 1450, allowed text to take centre stage as the elements making up pictures and graphics were too complex to systematize. It is only in the 19th century that new printing techniques made it possible for imagery to resurface on a mass scale with signs, maps, instructions, posters, icons, symbols, all kinds of product packaging, hazard warnings, and today it is all-pervasive.

Visuals communicate iconically as our brain perceives, encapsulates and deciphers image elements in simultaneous chunks whereas language and the written word is decoded in a sequential, linear way. This takes more time to process. Think of seeing a circle and you grasp it in one; describe it in words, it is a lengthier process, 'a curved line with every point equal from the centre'.

Imagery is omnipresent and its use is mounting with unprecedented growth from mobile pictures to Pinterest. Why? Our minds react differently to visual stimuli as we understand and remember them more easily, and images enhance the emotional response, affecting our decision making. The 'picture superiority effect' shows that concepts are much more likely to be remembered experientially with imagery. Not surprisingly the educational and advertising world has grasped this. Apparently over 80% of what humans learn is visual and more than 50% of mobile users watch videos on their device, and over half of all Internet users share self-generated visual content. There is also the often quoted apparent 'fact' that we process the visual 60,000 faster than text[15][16].

... the visual is beginning to dominate our sensory landscape and merging image and text via infographics will become more pervasive.

The rise in computing capabilities combined with advances in image recognition and pattern software linked to artificial intelligence and self-learning systems are making it easy to manipulate the visual. Websites like 'tineye.com' and its pixel to pixel matching software can extract endless information.

Images are packed with meaning and people think in pictures and unless words, concepts or ideas are connected onto an image they are rapidly forgotten.

Information and option overload additionally pushes people into the visual. There is also the additional power of infographics - a merger of visuals and text taking the best of text, word or letter icons and full images. Facebook always gets more 'likes' for photos even if they are trivial than for words.

The importance of visual literacy[17], being able to read, decode and understand the visual is crucial as is word based literacy, since verbal associations are better at understanding abstract concepts such as ethics and values. This narrative communication takes longer to grasp, but when grasped it sits more deeply.

The renowned creativity researcher Howard Gardner in 'The App Generation" explored youth creativity in the last 25 years. His team analyzed over 350 pieces of visual art and nearly 100 fiction stories written by middle and high school students between 1990 and 2011. They found that certain dimensions of creativity, such

COPENHAGEN
PARIS
MILAN
LONDON
NEWYORK
TOKYO
SYDNEY

HYDRAN

Sydney - Shop trying hard to be trendy, yet global cities are the communication hubs of the digital world.

as originality, experimentation and complexity, have diminished in the literary domain while they've increased in the visual domain. The literary pieces written recently tended to be more mundane exploring less with genre, character types and setting.

"A story from the early 1990s might involve a character who metamorphosed into a butterfly... there was little such deviation from reality in the more recent pieces... In the visual art there was increasing experimentation and sophistication... drawing on the expanding media at their disposal to create layered works that hold the eye longer with increased complexity and unexpected composition. Digital media technologies can support creativity by providing new tools with which to create new opportunities to share one's work with a wide audience."

... verbal creativity is declining and the visual imagination rising.

THE URBAN EXPERIENCE

The seductive city

There is a seductive quality and compelling narrative to this digitized city that sucks you softly into its interactive web where with a swipe and a click you can be gratified – mostly instantly. It can trigger desires so you want for more. This is a place with ubiquitous wifi, where we move easily between the worlds of 'here and there', that is the local, the global, the physically real and the virtual. Mobile devices give us this mobility so we can work on the fly, be up to date and where our vast library the Internet provides untold knowledge resources. This city communicates through every fibre of its being. It is dynamic: signs move, billboards tell stories, info boards inform. It has a filmic quality, you sense you are floating – somewhat. It does not feel static, and the buildings still have solidity even though their surfaces might move and their textures are more transparent as glass proliferates. There is a conscious orchestration of serendipity as meeting places and third places grow from the park bench to the café. This changes our work environments, with portfolio working becoming more dominant. The classic office feels constrained by comparison.

... the city communicates through every fibre of its being.

The digital spreads like oxygen with every social group participating, yet those operating 'on the move' and on a global scale remain the minority, with one large segment, the portfolio worker, representing just over a third of the workforce. Bus and truck drivers, nurses, shop staff, dentists, museum attendants or construction workers might have digital resources at hand but still conform to traditional work patterns.

Everyone and everything is supported by an invisible infrastructure of 'smart city' ICT that enhances the quality, performance and interactivity of urban services, from mobility to environmental monitoring and maintenance with self-regulatory systems. These mostly reduce costs and resource consumption and when done well they improve contact between citizens and government.

The sensescape of cities

The digitally enabled cityscape has provided the global brands that are present in all larger cities with the ability to dominate

our sensescape and visual experience as they seek to embed their distinctive identities on place. This has emotional and psychological effects on urban dwellers that are only beginning to be charted given the dangers of sense overload, clutter and over-stimulation. So some cities like Sao Paolo, Paris and Tokyo are now seeking to control this proliferation in the public interest.

Their increasingly sophisticated facades, illuminated signs and billboards, especially in their flagship stores with large LED pixel screens with high-resolution dynamic images, are at times interspersed with video screens as extra decoration. This is only possible with digitally driven media. A dramatic example of these innovative screens is in Times Square in New York[18], largely shaped by the Branded Cities Network: "We are a digital and spectacular media company with the most iconic signage in Times Square... which through "Brandscaping" focuses on providing unique solutions for brands to help them reach the ever-elusive consumer. Brandscaping is achieved by combining static and digital spectacular signage, with branded entitlements (plazas, parks and public spaces), product-purchase integration, mobile marketing, social media and other engaging technologies. Brandscaping allows brands to be experienced multi-dimensionally in a controlled environment, reaching consumers with entertaining elements that produce

New York: Times Square is the quintessential brandscape and odel for many to emulate.

instant results." Readers will know the NASDAQ sign or the ABC Supersign, the nearly 350 square metre electronic icon, known for its signature wavy LED ribbons and its curved ticker tape. Another is the American Eagle shop that transmits images of consumers acting up within the store on a screen just opposite it, allowing pedestrians to sit and watch these branded messages which make the consumer a part of the urban marketing strategy and brand identity. Times Square is the extreme, but large Asian cities compete well. Yet many cities would contain what they regard as visual pollution and feel 'brands' are invasive.

Art & commerce

Increasingly artists are used to create the installations and pop-up events that generate this urban experience. Here Louis Vuitton is a master. Its store in Bond Street, London, is exemplary with a changing cast of artists intrinsic to how it sells its merchandise. Not a store but a maison, it is conceived as if it were the home of a collector. A huge portrait by Gilbert and George reminds you that this is not an ordinary store. Best known perhaps is the deal worth several million pounds with Yayoi Kusama. Vuitton's 2012 collection was inspired by her polka dots. The window displays both in Bond Street and in Selfridges seen in 460 stores in 64 countries were invigorating. Previously, Damien Hirst was responsible for a bespoke medicine chest for the brand while Grayson Perry and Tracy Emin have both curated the bookshelf at its Bond Street flagship store.

Here we see buildings transform, occasionally with sudden subversive, temporary elements to keep attention with artists at the forefront and increasingly graffiti artists being commissioned. A good public interest project that was not about selling brands was the 'Ultimate selfie' winter project in Aberdeen[19] where over 100 people described their lives in slow motion without using words on 60 locations in the city.

... artistic inventiveness is shifting how we experience the city.

Night time is where this overall urban branding process has special power. In this overwhelming digitally driven sensory landscape, public entities struggle to compete especially in projecting useful information from transport timetables, pollution monitoring, weather conditions, events or alerts. Other public interest issues concern questions such as: How sustainable is the energy consumption of luminous facades? To what extent are luminous facades obtrusive and contribute to visual pollution and what should the guidelines and standards be?

The smart city

The 'smart city' notion has a powerful rhetoric and involves using information and communication capacities to the full to increase performance, reduce resource use and increase connections between the city and citizen. It was initially promoted by big tech companies who identified the city as a major market and bulk purchaser of products and services to make life more convenient, efficient, secure, self-regulating and predictable. Companies were criticized as they did not initially focus on citizen engagement[20].

Ubiquitous wifi is a basic starting point and we now find in many cities embedded sensors tracking movements, pollution or energy use. Numerous experiments exist including: Albertslund lighting lab[21] in a Copenhagen suburb; Eindhoven's intelligent lighting strategy that creates responsive streets and even helps dementia

Tallinn: Two young women at a conference - 'look what I have to show you'.

patients to find their way. The city seeks to be a global model of experimenting with light – not surprising since Phillips is based in the city. There is Amsterdam's 'Social sensing on demand' that allows citizens to provide feedback to the city on any emerging condition from potential flooding to broken pavements. Barcelona's 'smart bins' project helps garbage trucks only pick full bins as sensors communicate to drivers. Or the strategy of Paris to develop community and design challenges to rethink urban furniture from bollards to bus shelters, which are interactive. There is Vienna's creation of a holistic 'Smart City Wien Framework' targeted to the year 2050 cutting across all dimensions from education to the economy.

There are also poster child cities like Songdo close to Incheon airport near Seoul aimed at attracting global corporates which uses smart city technology extensively. Songdo is a clean, relatively attractive but somewhat lifeless emotional experience, with mock Dutch windmills floating on a man-made lake next to a classic science park environment. Nesta's 'Smart Cities from the Ground Up' is a good summary of initiatives from across the globe.[22]

The smart city includes the buildings within them, which are being reconceived from consumers of energy, water or electricity and producers of waste to a position where buildings contribute positively either by dramatically reducing consumption but also giving back to grids and the system. This maybe by solarizing buildings, creating roof top gardens including growing foods or inserting bio-reactive façade elements filled with water and green algae. Here CO_2 is pumped into the system so the green algae multiplies by consuming sunlight and CO_2. A processing facility in the bottom of the building gathers the algae and allows it to be siphoned off and used. This is cradle to cradle thinking in action.

The citizen centre-stage

The 'smart' word is slippery, in danger of over-use and exhaustion with cities twisting definitions away from its corporate origins in order to redefine how the 'Smart City' debate is conducted. 'Smart' immediately became contentious as it conjured up a potentially dystopian flipside of the watchful eye monitoring both things and people. Many cities reacted strongly in trying to put the human being rather than technology at the centre, emphasizing the 'smart citizen' and their abilities, aspirations and anxieties.

In essence 'Smart City' now means making the most of a city's human, technical and ecological resources to increase the quality of city life or 'doing more with less' and being clever in the process of using ICT. (Just to confuse issues there is also the popular usage of 'smart' to mean specific, measurable, attainable, realistic and time-related.)

Here Eurocities' CITYkeys project is illuminating. It is an attempt to create a performance measurement framework to monitor and compare how smart city solutions have been implemented. It conducted a significant survey to assess citizens' needs from a smart city.[23] Interestingly the scope seen by citizens is far wider than ICT solutions and the most important goal was 'the creation of innovation and knowledge' in general. Importantly only 11% of cities fully monitor their smart city progress and 39% partially.

The inherent promise of digitization and GPS technology is that we can re-create some of the social bonds, connections and interactions at a more local level. Eurocities summarizes well the perspective from a public interest view: "Becoming a smarter city is not an end goal, but a continuous process to be more resource efficient whilst simultaneously improving quality of life". Smarter cities are part of a shift towards openness in terms of data, interfaces, platforms and open smart city standards.

There are no one size fits all solutions: becoming smarter will mean different things to different cities. Most of all, it is crucial to involve people in the process: there can be no smart city without smart citizens. "Smarter cities should be inclusive places that use technology and innovation to empower, engage with and capitalise on citizen participation. Engaging citizens goes beyond the uptake of technology: it extends to the co-creation of ideas and solutions. Smarter cities can encourage this using new governance and transparency tools such as living labs, tools to integrate citizen input in urban planning, and spaces and support for start-ups. Successful smart cities will facilitate this participation, co-creation and co-production with citizens and other local partners."

The next word off the block will be 'equitable'. Most conferences, led by business or public entities are using the term as witnessed, for instance, by the Smart Cities Expo 2016.[25]

The pioneer

Many cities have for years looked to ICT to make management processes smoother, more efficient and effective. There is nothing special about that. The first city to grasp the potential of the connectivity and data revolution was Washington, DC with its 'Apps for Democracy' project of 2008. This was a game-changer and in effect launched the open data movement. Its Office of the Chief Technology Officer, Vivek Kundra, was the pioneer by asking iStrategyLabs a simple question: How could the city make its vast data catalogue useful for citizens, visitors, businesses and government agencies in Washington, DC. The catalogue containing all manner of open public data featuring real-time crime feeds, school test scores, and poverty indicators was the most comprehensive in the world.

The old way they thought – the Web 1.0 way – would cost several $million by outsourcing it to a single supplier and would probably not deliver a very good product. Combining with citizens' talents would be far more effective they thought. Only two rules applied, the first was to use the Washington Data Catalogue and the second to use open source with creative commons licensing so the results could be shared.

Their solution was the 'Apps for Democracy' challenge. The first edition contest cost the local authority $50,000 and returned 47 iPhone, Facebook and web applications with an estimated value in excess of $2,600,000 to the city. They included: A carpooling organizer, new biking maps, a 'We the People Wiki' peer-led community reference website that anyone can edit based on the public data, an application called 'Aware Real Time Alerts' on crime reports, building permits and the like. Many of these apps might seem obvious now, but were path-breaking then.

A follow up round the "Community Edition" looked for 5,000 feedback items with two aims: firstly to engage the people of Washington DC seeking their input into problems and then crowd source ideas that can be addressed with technology; and secondly to build the best system for receiving feedback and service requests via blog posts, email surveys, video testimonials, voice call-in captures or twitter updates. These events then launched the open data movement inspiring cities like Helsinki, Amsterdam, Barcelona and others to follow suit from 2010 onwards.

Foresight & weak signals

Cities need to remain alert to ensure their priorities and values are acknowledged as the digital industrial complex seeks to try to insert itself into urban agendas. Cities thus should create a 'thinking brain' put together from a mixed partnership and an agile organizational form that learns to understand weak signals on the horizon as well as nearer term predictions. What this strategic grouping and its relations might be, locally and globally, will differ in varied settings. Within the public sector the research and statistical departments could take the lead role, acting like reinvented super-librarians, decoding, analysing, interpreting, curating and explaining the evolving world. Their core knowledge-base includes data number crunching capabilities aligned to both analytical intelligence and research competencies. But more is needed namely the ability to think vertically - within a safe, deep knowledge-base - and horizontally, at the same time so able to cut across disciplines and forms of knowledge. That is to understand the essence of other disciplines so shaping the capacity to think comprehensively. But even more is required: an open mind that acts like a listening post and allows for the unexpected, whose feelers are tuned into 'weak signals'.

These signals, often hidden from view, may be snippets rather than clear, strong alerts. Like in a jigsaw puzzle the larger and smaller pieces need fitting together to see if they are simply observations of a novelty, an issue, a trend, a tendency or even a movement. And it may be time to listen carefully to the mavericks since many social innovations in cities have come out of alternative movements, such as guerrilla gardening or tactical urbanism. Note also Art Fry who invented the Post-it note or Finland's Matti Makkonen who invented text messaging, neither attracted people at first, until they spread from the margins to the masses.

The process of thinking ahead is changing. In the past our foresight was based on expert opinion and then on secondary sources such as published materials, data or market research. Now there is a third layer, social intelligence, where sharp antennae are needed to detect and interpret the flows of social media noise and conversations including buzz volume, discussion topics and crucially qualitative insights. This can give real time knowledge, radically changing the older pattern where 80% of time and

... the pioneers are often seen as mavericks, but take care they may be onto to something.

Krakow: He – definitely absorbed; she – either reflecting or bored with him.

effort was spent on gathering information with only a remainder on analyzing it.[26]

The power of new forms of insight, including data analytics and visual clues, but, equally importantly, cultural and visual literacy or business dynamics, change typical approaches to foresight and future-casting such as SWOT, scenario planning or Porter's 5 forces. These are now inadequate.

The overall aim is to search for grand patterns of social change and being able to distinguish between fads and fashion or noise and deeper rooted shifts and the occasional change that uproots the tectonic plates. Remember too that many things seem different but are the same in new technological clothes. For instance, crowdfunding is a version of what once was called public subscription or building an investor community.

... novel forms of analysis are seeking the grand patterns of change.

*Digitally created image that encapsu[...]
the question of trust in the digita[...]
(by K J Be[...]*

Some things we can predict with relative certainty, such as that artificial intelligence will have forceful impacts or robots a greater presence with driverless cars just the beginning. Yet have we collectively assessed their influence on jobs and unemployment and how whole classes of work will disappear. What then will our future job profiles be? Are we training the young for maths and sciences, but also are we considering whether we need more humanities in a techno fixed era?

This foresight function is crucial if we want to future proof our cities and adapt to change given the blizzard of information that thunders through the digital highways possibly cluttering our minds and obscuring clarity of thought. This requires a different mindset and a culture that dares to relax into uncertainty and ambiguity. It also requires a culture of experimentation as we move from planning the known in a predict-and-provide model to preparing for the unknown.

Deeper foresight that detects shifts across domains rather than simply along a narrow furrow, like technology, is rare. Yet Daniel Bell in 1979 was able to foresee the convergence of computers, TV, and telephones into a single system allowing data and the interaction of people and computers to be transmitted in real time. And in 1973 he coined the powerful concept 'post-industrial society' that sketched where we are today. (Ivan Illich also used the term in 1973). Indeed Ernest Mandel too in 1972 predicted how computing would create a third wave of industrialization. [27]

The collaborative imperative

The twin conditions to foster new solutions to problems and to harness opportunities are openness and collaboration. This is summarized well by Forum Virium (FV) which notes there are three options. First, each city buys its own dedicated and customized systems - this is expensive and inefficient but still the dominant model today. Second, large corporates produce service platforms and sell them to cities one by one with the city acting merely as a customer. "This is okay. When a large company sells a product to a hundred different places, as the 101st buyer the city will get a fairly good product. The downside is that these are closed source solutions." Being tied to and locked into one company as provider risks the city becoming an addict, even if that company may be the best. The solution is for a group of cities, companies and citizens to collaborate in building an open source service platform, on top of which different stakeholders can develop their own services. FV notes: "The great thing about using open source code is that it enables changing service providers, it lowers costs and allows small and medium sized companies get involved in public IT service development."

... silo thinking, planning and acting will never help us achieve a great city.

The aim is for cities to have interfaces that are open so they can communicate and learn. This leads to a next step - urban platforms between cities operating on common standards, as detailed in the Forum Virium-led Six City Strategy and Digiconnect, the European Union's memorandum on urban platforms.[28]

This collaborative model, based on openness, in turn requires a new governance model whose co-creation effect could be just as disruptive as Uber was to taxi companies. If achieved, it would imply cities getting involved in the innovation dynamic at an exponential rate. With cities as part of the innovation eco-system they would be able to hire experts on short, task-driven projects (like Digital Helsinki) and to be actors in the evolution of open data and its experiments, including new models of procurement such as giving start-ups privileged access, so force-feeding innovation and business development. Cities can therefore both be part of the innovation process as well as address austerity, equality and wealth creation issues. Such an integrated approach is not confined to big cities as Ghent, Tallinn or Riga prove with populations of around 200,000.

DELIGHTS & DISCONTENTS

The promise, paradoxes & predicaments

The digerati, that elite of the Internet, draw pictures and promote a vision of what could be and it can be seductive. Technology in this vision can be deified, so to be cautious about the digital is not to be a technophobe or luddite but fosters a healthy rather than headless attitude that encourages public discussion and reflection. It focuses on ensuring that the public interest remains in view. "Any process of major technological change generates its own mythology: 'Technologies of Freedom', 'The Network Society', and 'The Culture of Autonomy'. At its origins the "Internet is a technology of freedom, coming from a libertarian culture, paradoxically financed by the Pentagon for the benefit of scientists, engineers, and their students, with no direct military application in mind" (Castells 2001).

Technology and innovation are like a double-edged sword with digital technology ushering in a classic Schumpeterian creative destruction[29] period bringing into reach untold potential and the capacity to do old things better. Think of Wikpedia or Skype. Yet this can also threaten, be sinister and even destroy the valuable. Think here of the erosion of personal privacy and the ability of government to maintain an ever more watchful eye. And even the new mega-corporations, so seemingly hip, might in effect control every move we make in the digital world. Think here of Google, Amazon, Facebook or Apple. These powerful forces have increasingly been active in mobilising their customers to fight government regulations by launching crusades to shape the world in their image, with Uber and Facebook as high profiles examples. This reminds us that: 'whoever controls the technology to mobilise our attention will essentially set the terms of political debate'.[31]

Our society is a 'technopoly' where we idolize its feats. The cultural critic Neil Postman sums up the dilemmas beautifully: "Because of its lengthy, intimate and inevitable relationship with culture, technology does not invite a close examination of its own consequences. It is the kind of friend that asks for trust and obedience, which most people are inclined to give because

... the double edged sword of technology and creative destruction.

ons: A 1.8 km
g closed car
nnel of ever
anging moving
agery at the Fête
s Lumières.

47

its gifts are truly bountiful. But, of course, there is a dark side to this friend... it creates a culture without a moral foundation. It undermines certain mental processes and social relations that make human life worth living. Technology, in sum, is both friend and enemy."[31]

Openness & the innovation accelerator

The delights of the digital are enhanced by curiosity and openness. This is an attitude of mind and these are primary pre-conditions to foster innovation in any sphere. This has led to the 'open source' movement which has been powered by the possibilities of the digital world. The logic is simple: many minds crowdsourcing ideas from differing backgrounds can help solve problems or create opportunities by sharing research and resources. This has turbocharged potential.

Open source

There had been free sharing of software between academics during the origins of computing and the Internet, and is well-etched into its ethos, but the movement took off in the early 1980s when the Free Software Foundation was launched. It gathered pace when Linux, invented by Linus Torvalds from Helsinki, was launched, a freely modifiable source code and it hit critical mass after the Open Source summit in 1998.

... A tension exists between an ethos of openness required to drive creativity and its flipside a desire to protect.

The idea spread to companies who had vast under-exploited patent libraries locked in their vaults and realized these assets could be unleashed, but also wanted to solve tough new problems by crowdsourcing. GE, one of the first in the field, has an 'open innovation manifesto' which states: "We believe openness leads to inventiveness and usefulness. We also believe that it's impossible for any organization to have all the best ideas, and we strive to collaborate with experts and entrepreneurs everywhere who share our passion to solve some of the world's most pressing issues. We're initiating a fundamental shift in the way we do business." Henry Chesbrough who coined the term 'Open innovation' says it is a paradigm that assumes firms can and should use external ideas as well as internal ideas to advance their technology or put differently it is "innovating with partners by sharing risk and sharing reward."

With open source the world is helping you. It relies on collaborative activities between disciplines as well as breaking the silos. Indeed, genetic technology advances could not have happened without medicine, engineering and digital enablers coming together, robotics only works with GPS, and many successful ageing projects link health, social services and culture together. The same applies to sectoral partnerships as when the public, private and community realms connect to address complex urban problems like entrenched deprivation, developing new mobility or energy saving schemes. These only work by bringing differing skills and approaches together.

Sci-art & the digital

An example of openness is how at the end of the 20th century, a rapprochement began between the two great ways of exploring, understanding and knowing: science and art, often called sci-art. This has been given a boost by digitization. This process of 'boundary blurring' has now generated considerable momentum in bringing their joint insights and those of technology much closer together. This collaborative activity has provided fresh ideas, new forms of analysis, new solutions and products. The partnerships have enriched and maximised each other's potential especially for those working with digital media. Initiatives undertaken in various parts of the world in the last 20 years have succeeded in tapping the urge, felt by scientists and artists alike, to find new methods of discovery with often unexpected results when they explored the cutting edge.

A special focus for art, technology and science collaboration developed once city centres became a union of everyday consumption and spectacle, in effect turning retailing into a part of the entertainment industry. This often blurred the boundaries between shopping, learning and the experience of culture. This involved creating settings where customers and visitors participate in all-embracing sensory events, whether for shopping, visiting a museum, going to a restaurant, conducting business to business activities or providing any personalized service from haircutting to arranging travel. In this process many of new inventions were explored, just as with art installations, and often using vast interactive screens.

Crucially the merging of creative economy sectors, such as music, design and the audio-visual, with the world of ICT and apps is happening at a pace and migrating into the larger digital landscape. Together they are becoming one of the largest sectors of the economy with multiple effects on areas as diverse as logistics, bio-medicine or film. In short any field where tracking, interactivity, immersion, virtual reality and experience is required.

Experiment zones

Few cities have become a laboratory for new ideas or test bed experimentation zones and in order to exemplify the real possibilities and pitfalls of a digitizing world more need to be set up. A typical pharma or car company by contrast has an R&D department that tests its products both internally and with external user groups. Cities usually have no R&D department – and they should have.

There is a long history of special spatial development zones focused on physical regeneration, like the London and Melbourne Docklands Development Authorities, which have preferential planning laws and tax breaks. Other zones encourage economic activity, such as Shenzhen Special Economic Zone established in 1980 that helped turn a village into a 13 million city. Within this zone is an even more special one that aims to attract service industries rather than big box manufacturers like Foxconn, the producer of iPhones, which has over 300,000 employees in one factory complex on the outskirts of Shenzhen. Here there is no income tax for finance professionals, lawyers and the creative people it seeks to attract, as well as no capital controls.

Pilot projects have proliferated, such as the EU's Urban Pilot Programme or more latterly the European URBACT programme, but it is questionable whether they are enough, even though they have provided an enormous pool of lessons learnt in the last 15 years, covering themes ranging from abandoned spaces, circular economies, financial engineering, social innovation, urban mobility to city branding and disadvantaged neighbourhoods. Launched in 2002 and now in its third programme (2014-2020), it is the European Union's response to increasing demands for an EU Urban Agenda. Yet a criticism has been that they are too policy-oriented, that they remain pilots, and that they have had too little practical or systemic impact on the ground.

The European Union is responding and good examples of a new generation of EU-funded projects are the three lighthouse projects of 2015. TRIANGULUM http://www.triangulum-project.eu/ REMOURBAN http://www.remourban.eu/ and GROWSMARTER http://www.grow-smarter.eu/home/ It is the first time the EU is trying fund integrated approaches within the smart city agenda.

Living Labs

Cities need safe places to try things out given the escalating speed of digitally-driven innovations. A city or a neighbourhood rather than a nation is the ideal place to experiment, such as Kalasatama in Helsinki. They have more legitimacy with citizens and users and are closer to them since many inventions require behaviour change. Here two movements have hastened the experimental approach. The first is the rise of the Living Lab notion, a term William Mitchell from MIT coined as 'living laboratory' in the 1990s and the second the smart city idea. Living Labs have a user-centric and citizen driven innovation philosophy fitting the co-creative ethos of the times in seeking to turn ideas into practice in real life contexts. These have either been a physical facility where people leading normal lives test how effective a new technology is, such as in PlaceLab at MIT[32] or ExperienceLab at Philips[33]. Alternatively they can be Living Labs which are more like organisational arrangements for engaging multiple stakeholders in research and real life

BIG BANG DATA

...T, SELFIES AND SURVEILLANCE...
...TISTS AND DESIGNERS SHOW HOW THE
...A EXPLOSION IS TRANSFORMING
...R WORLD.

London – Big Bang Data exhibition at Somerset House: The arts mostly pre-figure the innovations to come as they encourage curiosity and exploration.

experiments. These emerged in Europe in the early 2000s. One of the most interesting examples is the City of Things project in Antwerp, which embraces the whole city. (see box). There are now 170 active members worldwide[34].

The social & the shared

Social behaviour and life has changed and so has the city. Every medium of communication changes the way we interact and each one has foreshortened and bridged physical or mental distance. The steam revolution brought us railways to connect places faster. The electrical revolution gave us the telegraph and telephone to connect across distance as well as radio and television allowing us to reach mass audiences and of course the car, with each invention surpassing its predecessor with novel features. The electronic revolution enabled the Internet. The crucial difference between electrical and electronic circuits[35] is that electrical circuits have no decision making (processing) capability, whilst electronic circuits do. An electrical circuit simply powers machines with electricity, but an electronic circuit can interpret signals, instructions or perform a task. Most modern appliances combine both. A washing machine has a plug socket, a fuse, an on/off switch, a heater and motor to rotate the drum. Yet the user puts in the desired wash cycle and temperature via a control panel that are interpreted by electronic circuits. Another feature is size — electronic components are very, very small and electronic communication is very, very fast. The question is whether this latest technology affecting social interaction is surpassing the rate at which we can adapt.

Each transformation has increased social possibilities - sociability grew with the ability to catch a train, to drive a car, to make a phone call. It has not declined with the Internet, in fact it has escalated and been accelerated by the possibilities of social media. The central question is whether and in which ways it has changed the qualities of our interactions. Does online social life, catalysed by permanent connectivity, complement our offline world by enriching our overall life experience or replace it, leading to some loss. Communication in the flesh gives us touch, feel, the tone of voice, body language, facial expression, visual cues and the chemical pheromones that trigger excitement and biological impulses — in short the physical and emotional. New software advances are increasingly seeking to mirror these senses, yet can the chemistry imagined be as good as the real? Perhaps shutting out emotional elements that can distort conversations is positive given the relative anonymity of the Internet. Crucially the Internet enables us to shift from communicating to masses to mass self-expression. No more a message sent from one to many, but messages sent from many to many with interactivity attached. Here senders are receivers and receivers are senders.

The desire for and necessity of community has not changed, but how it is expressed and is socially constructed has. It is less bound in the fixed physical spaces of traditional community limited to family and a few outsiders. The astonishing technical advances that have enabled us to move and be mobile, also allow a more nomadic life within which we affiliate and identify ourselves in multiple ways, defined more by and embedded in our networks than classic bonds. Networks define community in a nomadic world. This sits well with deep long-term trends towards individualism and a 'culture of autonomy'. Such a culture has been given extra power through the Internet and is still cradled within tribal instincts of the in-group and out-group based on interests, prejudices and culture. People look for and choose the like-minded or useful, forming networks of connection with relative freedom, or search for new connections such as through dating sites. Yet there are two flipsides as this can encourage a more "me centred' society as well as the rapidly increasing negative networks where racists, paedophiles and other undesirables can find each other more easily.

Autonomous more assertive actors or groups can be active in their own right, notes[36] Manuel Castells, less bound by the rigidities and power of social, political and media institutions. Creating and getting news that is not swayed by mass media can be liberating. This allows people to "mobilize and introduce new cultures in every domain of social life: in work (entrepreneurship), in the media (the active audience), in the Internet (the creative user), in the market (the informed and proactive consumer), in education (students as informed critical thinkers, making possible the new frontier of e-learning and m-learning pedagogy)... and the more autonomous... she/he is, the more they use the web, and the more she/he uses the web, the more autonomous she/he becomes". It is palpably clear that: "The large-scale development of networking as the fundamental mechanism of social structuring and social change in every domain of social life is not possible without the Internet".

Anytime, anyplace, anywhere

The significant deeper question about the Internet is why is it so compelling, so much so that it changes our social life rather than focusing only on its tools and technical capabilities or those of Facebook, Instagram or What's App. It power lies in its freedom, flexibility and fluidity. It gives users space to be, to interact and to work anytime, anyplace, anywhere and with seamless connectivity, immediacy and instant involvement. It chimes with cultural and economic forces that privilege impermanence, such as contract-based portfolio working as well as outsourced casualized labour.

Psychologically this free flow can be taxing since everything that was solid, stable and secure is in motion. People need physical place to anchor themselves in and place matters as never before in spite of our increased virtual interactions. The loud cry for authenticity harbours a sense of lacking. Facilities, such as a café, which the mobile worker or nomad needs, representing the 'authentic', 'real' atmosphere, are mostly provided by people who love their neighbourhood or street. Their individuality is the expression of who they are, that they give back to the community. When people feel they belong, as of right, and this could simply be a known gathering place, they feel like citizens. This is different from being loyal and attached to the branded experience of entertainment chains.

The power of place

Place matters in this shifting landscape as it provides anchorage, belonging, opportunity, connection and ideally inspiration. Here online and offline, cyberspace and local space combine to make identity, shape interests and generate a meaningful life where people are more at ease in the multiple dimensions of the web and its multi-tasking possibilities.

This has manifestations in the way cities work, are designed and navigated. The public realm, from sidewalks to benches, pocket parks and well-designed covered areas rise dramatically in importance as do third places, like informal cafes.[37] These are essential for community building where you can be communal yet homely but always with free wifi. You are neither home nor in an office where you talk, transact or work on projects or can be alone together in a small crowd as well as watching others. It is a neutral territory, a leveller of difference and an outdoor community or living room. Space distinctions between home, work and relaxing are increasingly blurring – a new space typology is emerging.

Cultural, social and economic imperatives and desires are driving the exponential growth of third places that have created multiple variants of the café, extending its scope from its historic origins in Turkey and the 14th century Mediterranean or its later popularity in places like Paris or London from the 16th century onwards. Always gathering places for social, intellectual and business life, now with laptops or tablets you take your work tools into the café.

The traditional office is in rapid decline, down by 33% in 2015 since its peak in 2009 when each worker had 35 sq. metres (now only 25 sq. metres). Greater connectivity and faster Internet have liberated people to work from home as telecommuters or on the move, and property prices have pushed corporates into reducing space. Third places are work environments both for stranded corporates liberated from the confines of a cubicle and the office tower and more significantly for the breathtaking increase in micro-businesses connected to the start-up culture, itself enabled by the Internet. Such spaces can be either commercial or co-operatively run co-working places or shared offices that both reduce costs and increase the potential for interaction across disciplines. For many, the rent-free café, the bookstore, the library, theatre foyer or publicly accessible lobby are vital since costs are minimal (bar the drinks bill).

Third places

A typical image of life in an Internet café is heads down, fidgeting and not looking up — physically present and absorbed in remote connections but not making social contact. Yet is this any different from being in a library in times past absorbed in a pile of books. There is simply a power in being alone together, so the social effects of the Internet on peoples' psychological well-being largely look fine.

The main quality of third places is being welcoming, comfortable, easy, accessible spaces, with a combination of regulars and newcomers, and where you do not have to spend money. As a bonus many animate their venues and organize diversions to encourage engagement, commitment and belonging, be that music, talks or poetry readings, exhibitions, fairs and food events. A whole street even gets involved on special occasions.

Indeed, the collective urban experience will take on added importance in future. With fragmented communication channels as the norm, there are very few common events to be discussed over the clichéd water cooler. Perhaps watching the football world cup or more locally the sports team where tribal loyalties can be expressed. This is why festivals culture and spectacular events, often artistically driven, frame an increasingly significant part of urban culture. See here the vast expansion of *lumiere* events across the world.

Seattle: A library massively used as a third place for work and pleasure.

... in an anywhere anytime world public gathering places become increasingly important.

Third places, of course, exist in the virtual realm with online communities, whose qualities mirror those of physical communities and where relative freedom from social status is a boon. You can extend your tentacles into cyberspace and be personal, approachable, or professional and communicate from the comfort of your home, university or workplace. Special interest virtual communities have been with us longest in academia, but the popularity of online multiplayer video games is revealing. They form global communities with social norms and rules of engagement similar to those of third places, such as giving regulars the role of moderator or special credit, even though they may be acting through an avatar.

The city reinvented

The look, feel and structure of the cities we have built reflect their time and purpose especially their economic organization and mode of production. Our built environment has been designed for how we lived and worked at least 50 years ago. The factory world of industrialism with a 9-to-5 day or shift-working and with clear demarcations between home and work has gone. This fostered functional zoning with living, offices and dirty industry in tidy separation and ordered infrastructure, based on hubs and spokes piecing the city parts together with roads and metros systems. Typically, there was a city centre with key functions, government offices, the main retail and dominant cultural institutions.

What happens in a world of anyplace anywhere anytime? What happens with portfolio working where life and work are meshed and the mobile is the main communication device so you can work while walking? Indeed, time spent online while on the move has increased five-fold in the decade since 2005, and time spent online overall for the average adult has more than doubled to 20.5 hours per week.[38]

The city needs to be both reverse engineered for the digital age as well as to create new infrastructures that live within its hard-engineered fabric. The key ingredient then is free wifi and it needs to be everywhere in trams and trains, on buses and in cars and walking down the street, in parks. Getting to work can be just as productive as being at work. Expectations of what the city provides increases too. People want sensing technologies embedded into infrastructures which tell them what is happening in real time so they can make better decisions (for instance to use a train or bus or a specific road). They want the infrastructure to respond to their needs and behaviour and in general to help create a low-carbon city.

Suddenly too the city centre is not the only hub. Anywhere can be one provided a cluster of basic facilities are nearby, such as a multi-purpose venue, a few restaurants, an incubation centre, individually owned shops, places for the community to gather or a market. A walkable environment easy to reach and with good connections to other urban hubs is key.

It will need places to reflect, relax and feel near to nature and, ironically, as the digitized world becomes more immersive there will need to be places where we pay to avoid wifi.

Encroachment & engagement

The capacity of the Internet to engage us in untold worlds and in force-feeding potential and opportunity is widely acknowledged as beneficial. The Internet invites but also invades us and thus a vast literature is proliferating on the social changes brought about by the Internet and whether it or the social media is good or bad for you. Think here of: *Born Digital: Understanding the First Generation of Digital Natives* by John Palfrey and

Urs Gasser; *The Shallows* by Nicholas G. Carr; *The App Generation: How Today's Youth Navigate Identity, Intimacy, and Imagination in a Digital World* by Howard Gardner ; *The Organized Mind: Thinking Straight in the Age of Information Overload* by Daniel Levitin or *The Flickering Mind: Saving Education from the False Promise of Technology* by Todd Oppenheimer.

Many highlight the negative, citing how it is breaking concentration, fragmenting attention, disconnecting from life and invading the mindscape and leaving people defenceless. One under-explored dimension is the genetic basis of the addictive qualities of the social media and our attraction to the flashing light landscape of the urban environment. Drawing on this the advertising industry adroitly lures us into its web and inserts itself ever more cleverly into our consciousness.

A bias to be social

There is a deep neurological and thus psychological and emotional basis and bias to our need to be social and to communicate including the 'social brain' hypothesis.[39][40] Humans like all primates rely on each other and need a nurturing environment to survive and grow given the length of infancy and ability to be independent. To say 'humans are social animals' is not a cliché but a profound need. Sharing food, caring for infants, building protective environments, relying on extended family networks to meet challenges, meant our ancestors gathered and socialized and eventually created the complex social lives of modern humans. It helps us understand the allure of the sharing economy. Social bonds ensure survival and what is now different between humans and non-humans is that our links criss-cross the globe through the Internet and they are explosive in reach and scale with a different quality.

...The saying 'humans are social animals is not a cliché but a deep-seated need.

That complexity has grown exponentially and how individuals, the social network and the group interact involves embedded chemical imperatives in the brain that help us understand the addictive power of social media. Everyone has experienced how it is impossible to ignore emails, to be compelled to Twitter or texting or to look up Facebook notifications or to have Googled information only to find you have ended up on a completely different topic.

Chemistry & curiosity

Dopamine plays a decisive role as neuro-scientists now understand how it effects mood, attention and motivation. It is like a curiosity drug. It causes 'seeking behaviour'[41] making us want, desire, search. This is critical from an evolutionary perspective as we need to scan surroundings and learn in order to survive, affecting not only basic needs like food, but also curiosity about things, thoughts and ideas – thus information.

Linked to dopamine, the driver of 'wanting' is the complementary 'pleasure feeling' opioid system.[42] One propels us into action and the other satisfies us and, crucially, dopamine does not have a saturation mechanism built in. This creates the dopamine loop as texting, Facebook, Twitter and the Internet can give you instant access to what is going on and instant response, rather like a conversation, or instant gratification. You seek, you get rewarded and this is where the addiction begins. You want more and more.

... wanting and liking creates the need for more and more wanting and liking.

This is heightened by the Facebook 'like' symbol which creates a process of emotional contagion, since we like to be liked. This creates 'intentional attunement' where by observing someone else's emotions the brain regions involved experience similar emotions in a mirroring process. This activates us to continue to respond, in a loop of 'unmediated resonance'

The reason people get overwhelmed by the power of the digitized world and social media are its very numbers. Dunbar's Number[43] suggests various limits. We can only have up to 150 people as casual friends or people whose name we know and might invite to a very big party. This cascades down to 50 people seen on occasion and then 15 people with whom you can be quite intimate and finally many surveys suggest that 5 is the number of our close support group[44]. So how can we handle 1,000-plus Facebook friends and 100s of Linkedin connections and Instagram followers. The answer is: with great difficulty and with psychological costs.

A set of studies by 'Anxietyuk.org.uk' and 'Anxiety.org' have explored the link between computers, smartphones and social networking sites and how social media obsession is linked to depression and anxiety. Most people use devices for socializing and keeping in touch with friends and family. Clearly an incredible advantage, but the headline grabbing findings are that 50% of regular users saw their behaviour change for the worse given

factors such as negatively comparing themselves to others or being online 24/7 – a major hazard especially amongst the young. 60 per cent felt the need to switch their devices off or using blockage software like Cold Turkey as they were not capable of simply ignoring them[45]. It seems that if you are predisposed to anxiety pressures technology acts as a tipping point, making people feel more insecure and overwhelmed and out of control.

The marketing armoury

Given this context, consider the communications armoury of the marketing world on a continual drive to grab attention. They know our weaknesses and how we move from one platform to another, always trying to stay updated and in the know and how in a matter of seconds we refresh Facebook feeds or pull down screen Twitter updates. But how do they circumvent the avoidance strategies, especially of Millennials[46] who long for the 'authentic' and where 60% think they see too much sponsored content and ads from brands.

To blast through the information saturation marketers do not need to create more information, but to make sense of what is already there. Stories are key in this context. This is how we think as humans seek order, certainty and narrative structures that are familiar,

... they know our weaknesses and feed on our insecurities and desires.

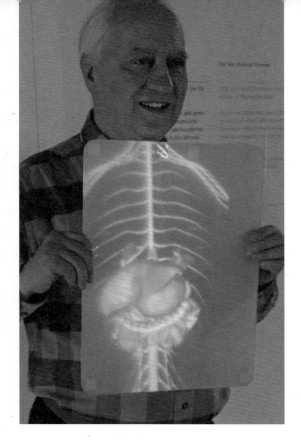

Linz Ars Electronica: Charles in front of a screen that can see his insides – digital sophistry at its best.

predictable, and comforting. These are ordering devices like settled mindsets, mental maps, scripts, metaphors, or narratives. Stories trigger parts of the brain concerned with imagination. Then we become participants in the narrative.

Users are now so focused on image-based social media platforms such as Tumblr, Pinterest, Instagram or videos that are growing exponentially, outpacing traditionally text-based media so the next move is 'visual storytelling'. These need to be monetized so videos get interrupted with

pre-roll ads that you cannot avoid. Ads need to get closer to the stream of status updates from the friends and influencers as this encourages the click-through rate. Ideally they are trying to integrate themselves into the update streams and into users' content so as to be noticed more. Here they invite followers to post/share/tweet/text content that frames a brand in a more positive light. We will see more incursions as marketers leap directly into Twitter streams as Twitter permits Promoted Tweets and Ad.ly enables celebrity endorsements. The aim to develop influencers who add credibility to a brand represents a dramatic change.

Storytelling

When these techniques are propelled into stories, invasiveness levels increase. Storytelling is the most powerful tool as it puts the whole brain to work stimulating a desire to connect threads and to narrate a causal sequence of events. This helps humans be able to extract meaning from seemingly incongruous and unrelated facts and data. Cognitive scientists believe human minds innately process and store incoming information as stories. Our sensory cortex lights up when urban screens, metro ads or online videos extol delicious foods or smells. Meaning and emotion then merge.

Gamification, which builds game principles into non-game contexts, such as competition, mastery and rewards, takes this a step further in order to improve the flow of the user experience and learning. It aims to create the infinite experience by allowing people to immerse themselves in a step-by-step process, so luring them into their web. Ian Bogost has called this marketing technique "exploitationware"

Controlling the self-inflicted encroachments of the digitized world cannot happen by decree and only works by discipline, by unsubscribing to newsletters and by shutting down devices. When the problems get worse the privileged protected wifi-free environments will definitely emerge just as we have seen with ad-free zones in cities.

There is a yearning for people to simplify the complex. There is a desire to find meaning in a world that seems to rush by. People long for tranquillity amidst the frenzy and fragmentary nature of everyday life. Reflective calm is something many search for and staying centred in this tech saturated world is not easy. No wonder 'mindfulness' is all the rage.

Civility & etiquette

The digital with its connective power is an unfolding civilizational force that inevitably shapes social life and behaviour and whose norms have not yet been firmly set. At the beginning of the mobile phone era people used to show off by letting their phones ring loudly in public places like restaurants and this rarely happens now. Yet, in Russia one can still hear phones interrupt a concert, but mostly putting phones on silent is the norm. In meetings or public lectures mobiles are ever present and we are not sure whether someone is on their private world e-mailing their friends or keeping up to date or tweeting or writing up notes. Are they paying attention or being distracted.

It is probably impossible to create strict regulations as behaviours evolve and are negotiated through practice so ultimately becoming norms or common sense values. So we have reached a stage where it is clear that the onus with mobiles is on the user to take the right steps, such as not to speak too loudly in public or put the phone on speaker, to know where not to use the phone, such as at a funeral or in a museum. The main point is to be alert since what is right in any given situation will be based on judgement.

GOVERNANCE & DEMOCRACY

The threads of the digital come together in considering the regulatory, governance and incentives framework that harmonizes well fairness, transparency, public access and the right to privacy.

This balancing act must navigate between sanctioning, enabling and supporting and containing, curtailing and controlling.

The two perspectives are: dealing with the core of the digital technology itself, such as standards and technology and then addressing the implications and consequences brought about by digitization, such as changes in social life or increased scope to be mobile. For instance, does the idea of citizenship change when we are mobile and have multiple identities.

The end of open-ended openness

At the heart of the Internet and the World Wide Web and at its origins lies openness and sharing and this has powered an intensity of interactions and opened up possibilities. This embedded trust was an accelerator of opportunity as it enhanced research capabilities, shortened transaction times, saved resources and even helps competitiveness. The 'sharing economy' largely relies on trust as do operations like eBay. The integrity of the person or organization, who lives what they say and the clarity and transparency of intent has created a trust zone. This is an operating environment which has had astonishing results, but it is under threat and the centralizing tendencies of the large tech corporates threaten the web's wide-open spaces.[47] There is a need for a new social contract of the Internet to regulate levels of openness and closedness and safety and security as well as to determine who is in control at one end and how to safeguard people from bullying at the other.[48] It includes addressing the ethics of digital databases.

We have lived through a struggle to open out data and more as of right, and much more needs to be done in the majority of countries. Yet with continuous tracking and the use of cookies, which remember your every move and then target you for

-lin: The
nificant Falling
ds Conference
lores what
ep-seated future
nds are.

advertising, a new level of invasiveness has occurred where privacy is more significant. In addition, personal data has an increasingly significant economic value for companies and social and practical value for individuals. Indeed, the World Economic Forum states: 'Personal data is becoming a new economic asset class, a valuable resource for the 21st century that will touch all aspects of society'.

MyData - the Nordic model

The *MyData* movement switches principles and is a paradigm shift in personal data management and in processing personal information, by seeking to shift the current organization-centric system to one where humans are in control. It is based on the right of individuals to access the data collected about them. The *MyData* approach aims at strengthening digital human rights, such as the right to be forgotten, while opening new opportunities for businesses to develop innovative personal data based services built on mutual trust.

The aim is to provide individuals with easy, practical means to access, obtain, and use datasets containing their personal information, such as purchasing data, traffic data, telecommunications data, medical records, financial information and data derived from various online services and to encourage organizations holding personal data to give individuals control over this data, extending beyond their minimum legal requirements to do so.[49] In similar vein Forum d'Avignon created a 'Preliminary Declaration of Digital Rights' in 2014 and is exploring setting up a Data-Ethical Culture Observatory.[50]

Reinventing democracy

Everything has been reinvented: business models, organizational forms, technologies and social life, but less so democracy. There is no shortage of ideas from deliberative democracy, which holds that there is more to democracy than simply voting or citizens budgeting. 'Beyond the Ballot: 57 Democratic Innovations from Around the World'[51] summarizes these well under electoral, consultation, deliberative, co-governance, direct democracy and e-democracy innovations.

Yet the full power of the digital unleashes untold abilities to mobilize opinion and movements, of which the Arab Spring, the Occupy movement, Five Star Movement in Italy and Podemos in Spain are current examples. The latter castigate the economic, political and media establishment and contrast themselves as speaking for the people. Tactical urbanism[52] projects, such as 'parking day', 'restaurant day', 'better block' or 'guerrilla gardening' stem from the same ethos. They are all social media savvy so enabling citizens to unite whilst not requiring them to meet physically. Their aim is to change the way the city and citizens communicate with each other and make decisions - these are the radical civics in action[53] and present some of the newer challenges to traditional notions of democracy from all quarters.

Harnessing community intelligence

Once you redefine the city as a community of brains where the aim is to harness the collective community intelligence there is a different paradigm. Historically community responsibility and its problems were outsourced to the public administration, which was a service production engine – 'why does the city not clean the streets.'

Consider how democratic participation is usually discussed where we ask 'have the people been consulted'. More important is how to harness people's capacities for the common good. Helsinki Region Infoshare[54] is an example of an enabling mechanism where people can play with data in a way that fosters entrepreneurship. This becomes a touchy topic when someone else than the city proposes to handle welfare services in a new way that returns the responsibility to take care of themselves back to the individual. Politicians find this difficult as they would be instantly labelled as wanting to dismantle the welfare society. However, the young whilst sharing the welfare philosophy are not wedded to preserving the model in its existing form.

Transparency & governance

All paperwork connected to Helsinki's decision-making procedures were moved into a digital environment in 2011. This Electronic Case Management System (AHJO) was initially used by several thousand users, from Councillors to City Board members and officials in city departments.

A game changer occurred when an open API (application programming interface) was inserted into the AHJO system in 2013. This made it possible for developers to innovate applications so enabling citizens to easily enter a formerly closed system and browse decisions, find related documents or track the course of a particular issue in the local political system. This works as each issue being prepared for decision-making receives a AHJO case number with the relevant metadata recorded for every step in the process. One prominent solution is the freely downloadable mobile app 'AHJO Explorer' used regularly by top decision-makers in the city as well as others.

Digital case management not only saves the public administration substantial resources, but more importantly it creates huge potential to govern more democratically and openly. Helsinki's open data policy was the backbone without which the AHJO system or the data portal Helsinki Region Infoshare where hundreds of open datasets are available for free use could not have happened. "My vision is that all the data on decision-making will be available to all", noted the Mayor Jussi Pajunen and strongly endorsed by the City Council in 2013.

Future ideas include the possibility to follow any issue already during the preparatory phase, browse all the data used as a basis for that decision-making issue and comment on the processes via social media. It is hard to imagine how Helsinki's decision-making system could be more transparent.

The break-up of established models of operating includes procurement, traditionally geared to lowest price rather than based on other principles. In encouraging new entrants, innovative procurement to encourage start-ups or SMEs is valuable.[55] In addition, *Citymart*[56] has explored how to transform the way some cities solve problems and procure by connecting them with new ideas through open challenges to entrepreneurs and citizens. This avoids those classic tender processes which are often focused on prescribed methods or technologies.

This raises the question of misalignment between digital natives' view of the world (new ways of doing things) and that of the digital settlers. Add to this that for the first time in history the young are teaching the old rather than the reverse. This is a dramatic shift with substantial cultural implications.

The context overlaying everything is that tax revenues can no longer pay for the service levels we are used to and this crisis is driving an atmosphere that things must change. On top of this, there are a series of 'revolutions' taking place.

First, the communications revolution has broken the monopoly of the public sector as everyone has access to knowledge on their devices and is able to be an editor of their own media. The combination of principle and technology have made transparency possible and there is no principled excuse for hiding - formerly you could claim a technical barrier and say: 'it is difficult to open data'.

Previously 'City' also meant City Hall and you would ask: 'why has the city/city hall not done this or that'. Now when people say 'City' they mean the whole community of people living in the city. This major upheaval of local governance means the City Hall has to support citizens' activities, with the community partially overtaking city government.

Feedback loops

The way the cities can operate is now much more transparent with instant, perhaps Twitter led feedback loops. 'The Twitter mayor', a deputy mayor of Helsinki Pekka Sauri exemplifies this. He started replying to citizens' queries by e-mail and found it increasingly inefficient as it was one to one. After a dramatic snow crisis and a mass of complaints in the city, he realized that the social media, one-to-many, and many-to-many communications increased his capacities exponentially. Five years ago regarded as a maverick, he now has 37,000 followers and regards the job of responding as *his job* rather than as an extra function to be outsourced to a department or external agency. However, some still ask 'when do you do your job?'. This implies a culture shift with transparency permeating the culture rather than in a flagship or figurehead project.

The open default position allows even the caretaker to use social media. If they grumble on internal matters (a constant fear), it means it has not been addressed in the department. Finally, can a city serve different people differently with custom-made services.

Brussels: Two digital natives in unison at play.

The mobile citizen

A mobile world where people move from place to place beggars the question 'where am I based and where am I a citizen?'. Nations and cities need to ask afresh 'what is identity' and 'what is citizenship'. Estonia that is 'so close to Russia, so far from Silicon Valley'[57] is an inspiration of where things could go. An innovation hub it has fully considered the consequences of the digital revolution. It regularly scores in the top ranks of the most digital, the most smart, or most innovative places in the world. It is one of the world's most digitally advanced places based on government strategies and support; broadband speed; cost and availability; wireless Internet access; technology adoption; with its records in the cloud; tech-education, technology culture and future potential. This is where Skype was invented, free wifi initiated in 2005, and e-governance has been launched.

It used a massive cyber-attack in 2007 as an opportunity to become the West's leading think tank on cyber security. It is positioning its digital strategy to push itself past its geopolitical constraints. Its e-residency programme does not extend physical residency, but allows anyone, worldwide, to establish a business in the country and to transact every aspect of their legal affairs online. Taxes can be paid, documents administered, notaries and intermediaries avoided, through using an electronic signature. In its first week it attracted than 13,000 subscribers. The aim is to give entrepreneurs abroad a stake in Estonia's future and indirectly increase the 'population' from 1.3 million to several million in the next decade.

MEASURING THE DIGITAL ECO-SYSTEM

There is IQ, EQ, CQ and now DQ. That is the intelligence quotient, emotional intelligence, called EQ, cultural intelligence called CQ and now the digital quotient DQ – the digital savviness of a business, place or city.

Measuring, benchmarking and evidence building is part of any solid management ethos. It rises in importance in transformational moments like the shift to the digital.

The notion of eco-system has become a mantra since it focuses on being holistic and it stresses the intrinsic interdependency and interactions of issues. Adapting Brilliant Noise,[58] a digital urban eco-system can be defined as a habitat, the digital platforms driving the city as a whole; communities, which are the public, private, community sectors and individuals, and their digital strategies and activities; populations which are groups and the influencers, activists and detractors within them; and lastly digital resources that are available to a city.

The methods to measure *digitality* or the digital capabilities of a city do not need to be conceptually different from good management sense, and various approaches exist. Three are highlighted, with the first two generic and the last city focused.

The first method *involves readiness, human capacities* and *performance*. It starts by looking at a city's digital readiness, such as whether it has a strategy, including a wish to be co-creative in moving to the digital world linked to a open-minded governance framework; then the presence of relevant digital infrastructures and a means of evaluating the city's progress. Second, it would look at its human capacities. These include: buy-in from leading players across sectors and their willingness to partner; solid competences downstream throughout the public organizations and other private and community entities; an open culture that fosters a test-and-learn culture. Lastly it would assess how a city is performing against desired and stated aims. These overarching criteria would be matched by many questions, such as 'is wifi ubiquitous' or 'is digital literacy part of the curriculum' combined with qualitative assessments such as, 'to what extent is the city *sensorized*'.

*ipei: Large,
ayful circuit board
blic art next to
e hip Huashan
the entrance to
ectronic City.*

69

A second approach has been proposed by McKinsey,[59] called the Digital Quotient DQ™ and is primarily addressed to the private sector, but its thinking can be adapted for cities. DQ™ assesses four major clusters that drive digital performance: *Strategy, culture, organization and capabilities*.

• Strategy – Is there a ambitious vision reflecting citizen needs and driven by them in place to meet short, medium and longer term digital aspirations.

• Culture – Have minds shifted and grasped the power of the digital. Is there a mind-set and behaviours able to capture digital opportunities by being willing to takes risks, to foster an agile experimentation culture and to encourage internal and external collaboration.

• Organization – Is there a structure and process with roles and responsibilities and appropriate skills and expertise able to implement a digital strategy.

• Capabilities – Are there technical systems, such as ubiquitous wifi, tools, such as data driven decision making processes or digital skills in place to achieve strategic digital goals.

Attached to these is a questionnaire-based qualitative diagnostic in order to dig deeper into the four domains.

The measures noted are strong in that they are simple, but weak in that they do not specifically focus on the sectors that make up an urban eco-system. The third method is the digital scorecard, and by contrast it can be applied to any sector such as health, environment or mobility and, most importantly, to a city as a whole.

Dublin's Digital Masterplan[60] launched in 2014 was the first comprehensive and pioneering initiative within which there was a Digital Maturity Scorecard (DMS) focused on the whole urban eco-system. Unfortunately, the city has put this holistic evaluation system on hold even though it would put Dublin at the forefront of digital thinking. It has scaled its plans back to focus more on tactical issues like delivering sensors for lighting, mobility, pollution and so on.

Yet the DMS provides the necessary broad-based conception that cities require to assess where they stand digitally and what they need to do. It defines six layers of digital activity that the city must build up to international and best practice standards in order to become a truly Digital City with a roadmap to match as follows:

'Digital city governance' includes: vision, strategy and management processes as well asan open innovation culture and novel procurement policies. The *'building ubiquitous city networks'* element includes interconnected, intelligent digital capacities. The 'leveraging urban data' component measures platforms, storage and analytics as well as progress on security and privacy issues. *'Fostering digital services' capabilities* looks at interoperability or levels of participatory design. *'Digital access and skills proficiency'* evaluates research capacity and digital inclusion. Finally *'city impact realisation'* assesses behaviour change, performance management or financial and non-financial returns.

Actions pursued as part of the Digital Masterplan relate to one or more of six digital city service domains which impact on quality of life in the city region: economy and innovation; community and citizenship; culture and entertainment; movement and transport; urban places and spaces; environmental practices. Within each domain there are also sub-elements within there are good practices that cities can aim for.

The scorecard looks at maturity on a scale of one to five. One is 'ad hoc' an unmanaged digital platform with little integration and insufficient skills. Level two is 'Basic' with a developing platform that has pockets of digital service innovation and limited citizen engagement and varying degrees of connectivity. Level three is 'intermediary' which is a somewhat progressive platform with citizen feedback loops and quadruple helix thinking embedded and a city data platform. Level four is 'advanced' with a proactive digital platform, integrated access, self-regulating intelligence and pervasive citizen participation. Level five is described as 'optimising' and digitally savvy, with ubiquitous networks, bottom up entrepreneurship and shared governance.

... the progress of the digital age can only be assessed by working across boundaries.

Digital Craft

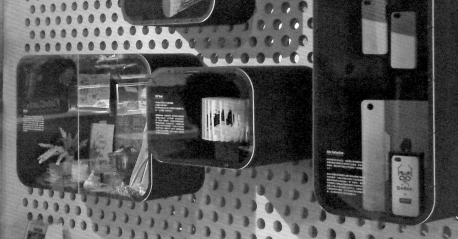

DIGITAL LITERACY

Literacy is the ability to understand, decode, work and create or communicate with the dominant symbol systems of a culture. Literacy, originally defined merely as the capacity to read and write with our alphabet system, has vastly broadened, encompassing even cultural and emotional intelligence.

Various forms of intelligence or literacies are required to become competent, capable citizens of a city, and how and what we learn is changing. They include taking in and grasping the media landscape or the shifts in and interpretations of a knowledge intensive society or the digital age itself. Literacy is a higher order form of thinking and acquiring knowledge, and requires more than fact and discipline based learning.

There is a digital deficit in Europe with approximate 90% of jobs requiring some ICT skills, yet digital literacy cannot be discussed in isolation. It is part of a bigger context namely the process and purpose of learning and knowledge acquisition in the 21st century. This is a political question. It concerns the purposes society chooses, which are negotiated in the public sphere. The traditional view of education's role was concerned with building responsible, capable, democratically-inclined citizens. The dominant discourse now is that learning should be primarily a servant of the economy[61] with knowledge as the asset, replacing location or physical resources. This is effectively the neo-liberal agenda with knowledge seen as use value feeding an engine to instrumentalize its worth. Currently it is cities that are pushing back on this narrow perspective. They are shifting the smart cities agenda with a focus on 'people first' given the complaint that corporates are using cities simply as a new market to sell the technologies for smart city solutions.

A central challenge for our age, given its extensive diversities, is to define the comprehensive cultural, social and personal purpose and ethos for learning in the 21st century. This requires a different story and a collective agreement that overcomes the dilemma and tension between fitting people into the dominant idea of a good citizen and worker and its more liberating role to help people discover themselves and their distinctiveness as they participate in a democratic society[62].

The concept of today's knowledge society is a complex shorthand for the fundamental qualitative changes we are experiencing in the digital age and are of the same order of magnitude as industrialisation 200 years ago[63]. Yet, the learning system is conceived and still largely organized for a past industrial age and those needs. It could be called a production line approach to mass produce standardized pupils ready for work guided within a canon of accepted universal truths. We now realize there are many truths, many forms of knowledge and so experts are less trusted. In addition, people have many identities and play multiple roles. Learning then changes and so should schools or universities. People will still be encouraged to understand the rules and knowledge of traditional disciplines, professions and trades, yet with an aim to see how they might be improved, applied to new situations, mixed in with different disciplines and replaced in an innovation process.[64] This shift explains the innovation frenzy that can be detrimental to achieving other forms of value and values.

Digital literacy is more than functional IT skills but a richer set of digital behaviours, practices and identity management processes[65]. A pixelated, screen based collaborative and participative world is dramatically different from one based on paper and type. The culture changes too. It shifts the focus from simply remembering, understanding and applying facts and knowledge to being able to learn to learn, to critically analyse and vitally to create and co-create. In short to live, manage oneself and operate in a digital society.

... digital literacy is a richer set of skills than merely knowing how to use smartphones and computers.

The obvious digital disciplines and practices we need to learn include using the diversity of social media, instant messaging and participating online, blogging, video or podcasting, searching, processing and evaluating online information, maintaining a website, *photoshopping* and so on.

The Digital Europe Agenda[66] notes that to be competitive and inclusive Europe's education systems - from primary to university level – need to transform systematically to fully integrate digital literacy into the curriculum. They identify three e-skill gaps starting with basic ICT skills, for instance also teaching teachers; second increasing the status of maths and science; and then

Bristol: City leadership summit autumn 2015 and new tech helps everyone participate.

preparing for job skills increasingly taught on the job itself and, finally, knowledge economy expertise, such as understanding the digital dynamic, which is critical for innovation. Europe's Internet penetration is 80%, but this masks a North/South divide, and anyway having an Internet connection does not mean you are able to use its potential. See here the recent World Bank research quoted in 'The Internet is not the equalizer'[67].

This is crucial given the strong correlation between e-skills and competitiveness. Notwithstanding the vital economic spin-offs from digital competence, much of the policy debate tends to overlook the deeper cultural learning required to adapt to the digital world as well as its pitfalls.

... deep cultural learning is needed to make the best of the digital age.

The requisite 21st century thinking and knowledge is different from that of the 20th century. For instance, thinking about thinking is crucial to the development of artificial intelligence, the next driver of the digital.

Knowledge is a resource and, to drive innovation, fields of knowledge can be mixed just as with the digital world which allows you to remix images, words and music. This means going beyond the mastery of a subject and requires the ability for navigational thinking which enables you to scan horizons and detect the essence, the assumptions and how experts generate their knowledge rather than its details. This higher order thinking, some call 'meta strategic knowledge' or 'meta cognition'.

"Knowledge is no longer a 'thing' or matter produced by humans and then codified in disciplines or by experts... it is more like energy, defined by its effectiveness in action, by the results it achieves... it cannot be defined, pinned down, stored and measured, but is a dynamic, fluid and generative force, or capacity to do things". Knowledge will be mobilized on an as-and-when-needed basis to produce innovative new products. (Manuel Castells[68]). This redefinition of knowledge has implications for what and how we learn.

Next steps

Digital technology is a revolutionary force and we need a guiding picture of what we want from its power as citizens and cities. This needs an ethical anchor to guide politics, policies and investment, which should be about solving the global and local problems that really matter. It needs to be driven down into new procurement methods, new collaborative technology sharing platforms, new regulatory and financial frameworks. These can push markets into the right direction and create the conditions to unleash a mass of small scale citizen, community or business led innovations that lead to massive change[69]. Without machinery and an engine that pushes the digital into public interest investment all we will get are the conveniences consumers want to buy rather than 'The City We Need' as the globally participative process launched by the UN-Habitat World Urban Campaign (WUC) spells out. In their 2012 Manifesto for Cities their 150 plus partner organizations stressed: *"the battle for a more sustainable future will be won or lost in cities."* Tens of thousands of people across the globe have subsequently met in events like the Urban Thinkers Campuses series and stated the obvious but necessary, that we need: well-planned, fair, more equal, safe, healthy cities that combat climate issues and provide opportunities to make the most of peoples' potential to enhance overall prosperity. And on inequality it should be remembered against the prevailing rhetoric that the technology driven economy is exacerbating our inequalities.[70]

Think cities, think digital technology and the smart cities moniker rises with force. Yet where are these smart cities so much talked about and which provide 'the city we need'. Places that are already possible to create technologically. There are pilots, short term initiatives, corporate R&D projects or grant funded experiments. There is little collective courage, will and determination from cities to ensure that every procurement from private sector providers has smart city criteria built into them, nor have planning, energy or building codes been adapted for the digitally enabled age.

Now is the time to become enlightened.

Let us remember technology left on its own can do more harm than good unless it is cradled within more lofty aims. As Rick Robinson notes in his insightful essay: *A Smart City or community is one which successfully harnesses the most powerful tool of our age – digital technology – to create opportunities for its citizens; to address the most severe acute challenges the human race has ever faced, arising from global urbanisation and population growth and man-made climate change; and to address the persistent challenge of social and economic inequality.*[71]

Periods of history involving mass transformation, like the industrial or technological revolution of the past fifty years, can produce confusion; a sense of liberation combined with a feeling of being swept along by events. It takes a while for new ethical stances to take root or to establish a new and coherent world view. The digital revolution is well underway and we now stand at the cusp of a rare and perhaps once in a lifetime opportunity to make cities better places with technology an able servant and enabler to allow citizens and cities to be and become the best they can be.

REFERENCES

1 https://www2.deloitte.com/content/dam/Deloitte/us/Documents/consumer-business/us-cb-navigating-the-new-digital-divide-v2-051315.pdf

2 https://eu-smartcities.eu/content/urban-platforms

3 https://www.accenture.com/t20150707T034708__w__/us-en/_acnmedia/Accenture/Conversion-Assets/Blogs/Documents/1/Accenture-Being-Digital-No-Regrets-2015-Report.pdf⁴ http://triplehelix.stanford.edu/3helix_concept

4 Jean Baudrillard Simulacra and Simulation (The Body in Theory: Histories of Cultural Materialism) University of Michigan Press 1994

5 https://www.google.co.uk/webhp?sourceid=chrome-instant&ion=1&espv=2&ie=UTF-8#q=tracking%20people%20hidden%20in%20recycling%20bins

6 http://www.bbc.co.uk/news/technology-14306146

7 http://www.bloomsbury.com/uk/digimodernism-9781441175281/#sthash.N8Z1PlUp.dpuf⁹ http://www.theguardian.com/environment/2008/mar/23/freiburg.germany.greenest.city

8 http://www.thescavenger.net/media-a-technology-sp-9915/61-mediatech2/73-postmodernism-is-out-digimodernism-is-in.html

9 http://idcdocserv.com/1678   10 hInternational Data Corporation https://www.idc.com/

11 Mark Andreessen co-founder venture capital firm Andreessen-Horowitz and co-founder of Netscape.

12 http://cbi.hhcc.com/writing/the-myth-of-5000-ads/

13 http://www.telegraph.co.uk/news/science/science-news/8316534/Welcome-to-the-information-age-174-newspapers-a-day.html

14 John Berger, Ways of Seeing (Penguin Books, 1972)   15 http://www.citedudesign.com/fr/home/

16 http://www.salonedelgusto.com/en/

17 https://www.adobe.com/content/dam/Adobe/en/education/pdfs/visual-literacy-wp.pdf A useful primer on visual literacy

18 http://www.timessquarenyc.org/advertising-sponsorships/digital-screens-billboards/index.aspx#.VoJ9rRWLSXs

19 http://www.bbc.co.uk/news/uk-scotland-35131344

20 http://www.theguardian.com/cities/2014/dec/17/truth-smart-city-destroy-democracy-urban-thinkers-buzzphrase

21 http://www.allledlighting.com/author.asp?section_id=560&doc_id=563367¹⁶ http://www.salonedelgusto.com/en/

22 https://www.nesta.org.uk/sites/default/files/rethinking_smart_cities_from_the_ground_up_2015.pdf

23 http://nws.eurocities.eu/MediaShell/media/CITYkeys%20-%20D1.1%20-%20Cities%20and%20citizens%20needs.pdf

24 http://www.eurocities.eu/eurocities/documents/EUROCITIES-statement-on-smart-cities-WSPO-9WQDQ9

25 http://www.smartcityexpo.com/program

26 http://www.mckinsey.com/insights/high_tech_telecoms_Internet/how_social_intelligence_can_guide_decisions

27 http://www.versobooks.com/books/612-late-capitalism

28 http://www.forumvirium.fi/en/sixpackstrategy https://ec.europa.eu/dgs/connect/en/content/dg-connect

29 http://economics.mit.edu/files/1785

30 http://www.theguardian.com/technology/2016/jan/03/hi-tech-silicon-valley-cult-populism

31 http://www.theguardian.com/technology/2012/dec/23/creative-destruction-john-naughton-networker

32 http://web.mit.edu/cron/group/house_n/placelab.html

33 http://www.theguardian.com/technology/2016/jan/03/hi-tech-silicon-valley-cult-populism

34 http://www.openlivinglabs.eu/aboutus

35 http://www.brightknowledge.org/knowledge-bank/engineering/careers-in-engineering/electrical-and-electronic-engineering-whats-the-difference

[36] https://www.bbvaopenmind.com/wp-content/uploads/2014/04/BBVA-OpenMind-book-Change-19-key-essays-on-how-Internet-is-changing-our-lives-Technology-Internet-Innovation.pdf

[37] Ray Oldenburg, The Great Good Place : Cafes, Coffee Shops, Bookstores, Bars, Hair Salons, and Other Hangouts at the Heart of a Community, Pegasus, 1999

[38] http://stakeholders.ofcom.org.uk/binaries/research/media-literacy/media-lit-10years/2015_Adults_media_use_and_at titudes_report.pdf

[39] http://kreativproces.dk/http:/kreativproces.dk/wp-content/uploads/2010/08/Dunbars-tal-og-reseach.pdf

[40] https://blog.bufferapp.com/psychology-of-social-media

[41] Susan Weinschenk http://www.blog.theteamw.com/2009/11/07/100-things-you-should-know-about-people-8-dopamine-makes-us-addicted-to-seeking-information/

[42] Kent C Berridge and Terry E Robinson http://thebrain.mcgill.ca/flash/capsules/pdf_articles/dopamine.pdf

[43] http://www.theguardian.com/technology/2010/mar/14/my-bright-idea-robin-dunbar

[44] hhttp://kreativproces.dk/http:/kreativproces.dk/wp-content/uploads/2010/08/Dunbars-tal-og-reseach.pdf

[45] hhttp://getcoldturkey.com/

[46] hhttp://socialmediaweek.org/blog/2015/09/better-with-millenials/

[47] http://www.ted.com/talks/tim_berners_lee_a_magna_carta_for_the_web?language=en

[48] http://www.huffingtonpost.com/jeanchristophe-nothias/the-new-social-contract-for-the-Internet_b_6273976.html

[49] hhttp://www.lvm.fi/documents/20181/859937/MyData-nordic-model/2e9b4eb0-68d7-463b-9460-821493449a63?version=1.0

[50] http://www.ddhn.org   [51] http://core.ac.uk/download/files/34/30511.pdf   [52] http://www.ddhn.org

[53] Tactical Urbanism: Short term action for long term change, by Mike Lydon and Anthony Garcia, Island Press, 2015

[54] http://www.hri.fi/en/

[55] file:///C:/Users/Charles/Downloads/Public-Procurement-Driver-of-Innovation.pdf

[56] http://www.citymart.com/blog/2014/9/24/citiesshare-session-3-overcoming-procurement-barriers

[57] http://www.realclearworld.com/blog/2015/01/estonias_digital_strategy_takes_center_stage_110887.html

[58] http://brilliantnoise.com/blog/the-digital-ecosystem

[59] http://www.mckinsey.com/client_service/mckinsey_digital/digital_quotient http://www.mckinsey.com/insights/or ganization/nine_questions_to_help_you_get_your_digital_transformation_right

[60] http://digitaldublin.ie/masterplan/ & http://digitaldublin.ie/two-innovative-toolsets/

[61] Jane Gilbert http://www.nzcer.org.nz/nzcerpress/catching-knowledge-wave-knowledge-society-and-future-education

[62] Ditto as above   [63] http://www.ddhn.org

[64] https://www.marxists.org/reference/subject/philosophy/works/fr/lyotard.htm

[65] https://www.jisc.ac.uk/guides/developing-digital-literacies   [66] http://issuu.com/monitortv/docs/digitaleurope

[68] hManuel Castells' The Rise of the Network Society quoted in http://nzbooks.org.nz/2006/non-fiction/waving-or-drowning-brian-opie/

[69] http://www.massivesmall.com/

[70] Andy McAfee and Erik Brynjolfsson in: https://www.foreignaffairs.com/articles/united-states/2014-06-04/new-world-order

[71] http://theurbantechnologist.com/2016/02/01/why-smart-cities-still-arent-working-for-us-after-20-years-and-how-we-can-fix-them/

'Charles has captured a rich story of the dramatic changes that will affect us all through digitization and tells it in a clear and compelling way.'

Pekka Sauri
Deputy Mayor
Helsinki

'The Digitized City is one of the fullest accounts of the ways cities will (or will not) get transformed by the ongoing technology and innovation revolution. This new city is full of benefits but also dangers, the smart and digitized city concept is, at the same time, an opportunity that cannot be skipped!'

Nikolaos Kontinakis
Project co-ordinator knowledge society,
Eurocities, the leading city network in Europe